1

Copyright © 2018 Tom Chapman Ltd
Cover design by Mark Elmer
& Willian Wamosy
Edited by Kimberley Parker
www.thelionsbarbercollective.com
tomchapmanhair@gmail.com

The advice and strategies found within may not be suitable for every
situation. This work is sold with the understanding that neither the
author, the interviewees nor the publisher are held responsible for
the results accrued from the advice in this book. The words and
opinions of the interviewees are their own.

ISBN-13: 978-1979930581 ISBN-10: 1979930589
BISAC: Biography & Autobiography / Business

I would like to express my gratitude to the many people who saw me through this book; to all those who provided their time, support, talked things over, read, wrote, offered comments, and assisted in the editing, proofreading and design. Mostly Kimberly Parker for her tireless editing and support, and the interviewees who gave up the time and knowledge to make this book what it is. I appreciate that time is the most precious commodity we own, so I am eternally grateful for their input. Above all I want to thank my wife ,Tenneille, and the rest of my family who supported and encouraged me in spite of all the time it took me away from them – like at this very moment sat in a coffee shop trying to perfect the art of self-publishing. It was a long and difficult journey for them as well as myself. Thank you. Thank you to the best neighbours in the world, Mark and Tash for always being there. I would like to thank Dom Lehane for inviting me back on to his podcast to discuss the book and for showing his interest in the project throughout, Simon Richie at Barber NV Magazine for promoting the book during the months leading up to the publication, and Rachel Gould at Modern Barber for writing the foreword as well as her ongoing support in my career and always being there for advice, it means an awful lot to me. Andrew Brewster of Barber Evo Magazine for his support with The Lions Barber Collective and publishing many of my images. Grant Northover of Phab Wholesale for giving me the opportunity to become an educator. Last and not least: Thank you to everyone who has ever given me a chance, an opportunity, or believed in me. I am fully aware that nobody 'makes it' alone and although I have a long way to go yet, I will be forever grateful for those who have been part of my journey. Without those people I would be nowhere and those whose names I have failed to mention, you know who you are.

Foreword

I made an early connection with Tom Chapman in the first few months of launching the *Modern Barber Magazine* and I was lucky enough to be the first to publish his work.

Over the years I've watched Tom channel his creativity and irrepressible energy beyond barbering and into the founding of The Lions Barber Collective. The Lions is an idea forged in Tom's kind heart and one that has reached to touch the lives of many, both inside the industry and out.

His wide network that spans the globe has uniquely placed him as the perfect author for a book such as this. *The Barber Boom* is thoughtfully researched and carefully structured to give the reader deep insight into varied perspectives on our thriving industry. Each interview is bookended with Tom's own personal comments and places each interviewee in context for the reader. I particularly loved the advice each professional shared which could easily be applied to anyone in any field seeking to reach the top of their game – keep pushing, never give up, stay focused, never stop learning, and surround yourself with good people…good people like Tom Chapman.

Rachel Gould - Modern Barber Magazine

Preface

This book started as a dream and has now come to life once I decided to just pick up my laptop and start typing, before I even had an idea. Then it came to me, I intended to chronicle my journey as a barber for a year. But then there was much more to it than that. My mission became simple: to try and find out why there has been such a rise in the popularisation of barbering. Throughout my journey I was fortunate enough to meet incredible people from all areas of the industry, and was able to find out more about not only their opinions, but also what led them to where they are today and the wisdom they've gained along the way.

My journey took me all over the globe, grabbing interviews serendipitously as and when I could with those who were kind enough to make time for me. As such the book is chronologically ordered, and interviews are of varying length depending on the individual. All interviewees were asked the same set of questions, along with some varying additions when the interviewee went in an interesting direction I felt would benefit the book. Interviews are presented in their original entirety as much as possible. Not only is this book intended to explore the 'barber boom' and the reasons behind it, I also intended it to be a kind of self-help manual. With a combined career knowledge of well over 100 years there must be a lesson or two to learn along the way.

CONTENTS

INTRODUCTION   8

DIFFERENT TYPES OF BARBERS   11

A BRIEF HISTORY OF BARBERING   16

MY JOURNEY   19

INTERVIEWS

Dan Davies   25
Jonathan Tayloni   34
Andrea Lynne Raymond   39
David Hildrew   44
Juan C Ramos   49
Eric Begg   55
Mike Taylor   61
Aileen Nuñez   67
Erin Wentworth   73
Paul Nicholson   79
Sam Wall   85
Robert 'Bert' - Jan Reitveld   90
Farad Salehi   99
Mark Peyton   106
Ollie Nobbs   117
Carl Blake   127
Alan Beak   133
Kieron Price   141
Lawrence Fo   147
Sindi Devitte   153

NEW BEGINNINGS   164

FINAL THOUGHTS   172

Introduction

It's the eve of my first tour of the USA and I'm sat alone in a generic hotel room near Heathrow airport, planes flying past my window every five minutes. During my teens and mid-twenties, one of my dreams was to tour the states as a rock star. At the time I was the front man in a metal band, and the prospect of being on stage in front of crowds of people from the other side of the world thrilled me. The romantic, rebellious rock 'n' roll lifestyle intrigued me. I hungered for it. At that point in my life my career always came second to the band – my focus was entirely on playing, writing and performing music. Little did I know that in 7 years' time I would be writing this introduction, preparing for a weeklong tour of the states of Nevada and California. Only it's not as the fake blood spitting, face-paint wearing front man of a metal band, No Such Thing As A King. It's as a barber.

It's no secret the barbering industry has exploded in the last few years. I regularly have people coming to me in person, messaging me through social media, and emailing me by the dozen. They're all asking me one thing: how can they get into barbering? There's been huge growth in the popularity and exposure of the industry, and with that an increased amount of interest and desirability to join it. This has led to barbering having its own subculture (I mean, Ive even been told I look like a barber. What the hell does that mean?), being featured more in media (particularly online), being respected for its skill, and in general being viewed as a fashionable and desirable career choice. For most of us who've been in the game for a while, this is more than we could've ever hoped for.

It made me think back to the beginnings of my career. At the time I was studying for my A Levels, and when I let my teachers know my future plans they were not encouraging in the slightest. They were disappointed in my choice and believed I should be headed to university. I got the distinct impression they viewed the career negatively. When I began my apprenticeship this opinion was even mirrored by the staff. For me however, I was doing something I wanted to do. I loved the creativity, camaraderie, and community involved. I also enjoyed getting to know the person in the chair and ensuring that they left feeling great. It was a perfect fit. I felt sorry for some of the guys I knew who felt pressured to go to University and study something they had no passion for. Unfortunately just because I saw barbering as being a successful and fulfilling career it didn't mean the rest of society (or even the rest of the hair industry) did.

That was nearly 15 years ago and thankfully a lot has changed since then. The standard is rising, the opportunities are growing, and barbering is finally becoming recognised as the serious, skilled profession it is. So the big question is…what changed? That sentiment is at the heart of why I'm writing this today and why I've decided to dedicate the next year to this project.

By the end of this book I hope to have explored some of the reasons behind the huge growth in the barbering. I figured the only way to do this was find the experts and ask them – and who knows more about the 'barber boom' than the barbers themselves? I want to get the perspective of all types of professionals, from educators to ambassadors, experienced veterans to rising stars. Through these interviews I hope not only to get their perspective on the 'barber boom', but also to know their backstory, and if they have advice for aspirational barbers-to-be. I want to have a better understanding of the barbering culture as whole, and delve deeper into the people who live it every day.

I've decided to have a simple set of questions, allowing the interviewee to expand wherever they feel appropriate:

1. What is your backstory and how, when, and why did you get into the industry?

2. When did the 'barber boom' begin and what's your opinion of it?

3. Do competitions matter and who do you think is the best barber?

4. What are your favourite products, tools, publications and events?

5. What effect does social media have on your career, and on barbering as a whole?

6. What advice do you have for prospective barbers?

The 'barber boom' is here and I've made it my mission to find out why.

"A barber (from the Latin barba, "beard") is a person whose occupation is mainly to cut, dress, groom, style and shave men's and boys' hair. A barber's place of work is known as a "barber shop" or a "barber's". Barber shops are also places of social interaction and public discourse. In some instances, barbershops are also public forums. They are the locations of open debates, voicing public concerns, and engaging citizens in discussions about contemporary issues. They were also influential in helping shape male identity."
(Source Wikipedia)

Different Types of Barbers

There's no denying that the 'barber boom' is well and truly upon us. The industry is bigger than ever, but barbering is no new business – in fact this trade goes back thousands of years. The barbering world was not always in such good favour; it was not that long ago that it was pretty much dismissed in the world of hairdressing. There were hardly any products dedicated to men/barbershops, no events, and no publications. That world was reserved for the professional hairdresser alone. In recent times barbers have finally begun to take men's hair back, finding their way into the spotlight. There's experimentation, creation of new styles, innovative products and tools, better education, standardisation, and recognition. Hairdressers are looking to barbers for advice on how to better their techniques in certain areas because they have noticed the fall in custom due to current trends and lack of education – there are even celebrity barbers and authors.

Over the thousands of years since the inception of barbering more and more different types of shops have appeared as it has evolved. I've identified a few varieties that I see as the most influential in the 'barber boom' :

Traditional

The 'Traditional' barber bases their shop around the style and ethos popularised during the first half of the 20th century. Their aim is to give their clientele classic services in an old-school environment – walnut furnishings, tiled floors, and plush leather chairs. They offer hot towel shaves (which are a staple of this type of business), a walk-in-and-wait system, and a friendly atmosphere. There might even be the offer of a libation. The standard and style of barbering obviously differs from 100 years ago as tools, equipment, and male fashion have developed a great deal since then, resulting in the highest quality haircuts but the atmosphere remains the same. Think of it almost like a gentleman's club.

Afro

Another prominent type of barbering is the afro-style. These shops have a strong culture all of their own and are hugely important their community. They hark back to a time when the barbershop was the place for men to gather, discuss ideas, and support each other and thats never gone away. It's not just a place to cut hair; these shops influence, unite, and creates a sense of togetherness. With such a strong effect on society it's promising to know that many shops take on this responsibility and respond positively – such as the recent initiative in the states for barbers to offer blood pressure readings.

Not only are these barbers doing great things for their community, they've also hugely influenced the 'barber boom' all over the globe. They basically invented and perfected fading and shape-ups, which are hugely popular and a huge influence on the barber boom. It is proof of the high skill level involved in this profession.

Men's Hairdressers

Men's Hairdressers specialise in male hair and are usually colour trained – something you don't tend to find in most traditional barbershops. Colouring men's hair has become increasingly more fashionable over the last 20 years. This became really popular again in the late 90s inspired by David Beckham's golden highlights, moving onto to the bright colour blocking popular around a decade ago, and finally with the current trend of silver/grey colourisation we see today. Men's hairdressers are able to achieve these looks thanks to their specialised experience in colour.

This type of barber is more comfortable with scissors and styling than with clippers. Being part of the salon environment they'll often wash the hair of each client and work from wet to dry, using a lot of products and finishing each cut with a blow dry. They'll work to appointment and offer drinks, head massages etc. They also tend to charge more and allocate more time for each client.

Military Barber

The military style barber spends their time completing a high volume of standard haircuts in short space of time. I recently visited one such barber in Canada – as soon as the shop opened the place was packed, with a queue reaching all the way around the shop and out onto the street. It was a walk-in system and their main work consisted of buzzcuts, flat tops, high and tights, and jarheads. The implementation of the rotary motor clippers excels in this kind of environment, thanks to its powerful motor, efficiency, and speed. It's safe to say you'll never see a faster, more precise flat top than in a Military Barbershop.

Modern Barber

Finally there's the 'Modern Barber', a hybrid developed over the last decade. This type of barber combines elements of all of the above, creating an experience that aims to offer the best of all barbers:

> **The Men's Club Vibe**
> Taken from the afro and traditional barbers, the Modern Barber attempts to replicate the friendly social atmosphere and camaraderie that makes shops the centre of their community. There has been a rise in 'men's only' barbershops which reflect this ethos – Schorem being a perfect example.

> **The Luxury**
> The luxurious indulgence involved in hair services is often seen as something only available at the salon. Not so for the Modern Barber. This isn't necessarily a new thing – after all a traditional towel shave is a wholly indulgent experience – however Modern Barbers are expanding their services even further. This might mean a face mask, wax, or even a manicure.

> **The Fade**
The recent popularity of the fade has meant the Modern Barber must have it in their skill set. It has had a huge impact on the industry as a whole – I spend 90% of my time as an educator teaching my students (mostly hairdressers) how to perfect it. This style has completely changed the game, requiring barbers to have a high level of precision and technique. It has also influenced the tools available as clippers companies have had to develop new technology to improve the quality of fades. This is all due to the expertise and influence of the afro barber.

> **The Hairdresser**
The influence of the Hairdresser has become more apparent in the last year or so, with many barbers dedicating time to styling and finishing to a high standard. This is something the Modern Barber also tries to implement, meaning there's an increase in hairdryers, straighteners, brushes, and male-specific wet line products in the shop.   To see the use of a small round brush in the barbering world to create new styles is fantastic. When I began my career it was only used for the dreaded 'sausage roll' blow-dry, so to see them being used by the likes of Alan Beak onstage at The Great British Barber Bash is brilliant. The boundaries between hairdressing and barbering have been broken down, allowing the hair industry to evolve into something new – the Modern Barber embraces that.

> **The Marketing**
A huge part of the Modern Barber's success is related to how they market themselves. Knowing how to use social media correctly, having a good camera, and creating a strong online network are all essential to the Modern Barber raising their profile. Not only that it connects individuals from all around the globe, making it easier to get inspiration and make connections.

The Modern Barber is a product of the 'barber boom', and is constantly evolving with it. Who would have thought that the DSLR camera would become such an important and common tool in the barbers arsenal? They are a symbol of a postmodern society in that he/she borrows traits from all those who have come before and paved the way. This move towards inclusion, acceptance, and recognition can only be a positive thing.

A Brief History of Barbering

Barbering is an ancient trade dating back as far as 3500 BC. With such a long and rich history the role of the barber has understandably altered a great deal over time. Unfortunately we don't have the time to explore the evolution of the barber fully – that merits its own book. We can however skip through the centuries for a brief overview.

Ancient Egypt

The first pit stop on our tour of barbering history is ancient Egypt. At this time barbers were extremely respected member of society, often being priests or healers. Hair was seen as a psychical representation of your thoughts, so a haircut was a way to cleanse yourself of evil or negativity. It's for this very reason priests used to shave themselves from head to toe every 3 days.

The Roman Empire

The trade continued to grow during the Roman Empire – the word barber actually comes from the Latin 'barba' which means beard. During this period a visit to the 'Tonsor' (barbershop) was an important part of the Roman male's routine, right up there with public baths. They were seen as a place to socialise with your peers, discussing everything from politics to philosophy and community issues. This was also the time when barbers began performing tooth extractions as an additional service.

The Middle Ages

By the time the Middle Ages came barbers had acquired additional roles of both surgeon and dentist, they were barber surgeons. Popular services you could get alongside your hair cut included trepanning, bloodletting, enemas, and leeching. Trained physicians preferred to study medicine at universities or take up residence with wealthy families, so barbers often found themselves employed on the battlefield. In fact even the father of modern surgery, Ambroise Pare, began his career as a barber surgeon.

By the mid-1500s English barbers were banned from providing surgical treatments, but remained part of the same trade guild as their surgeon brothers until 1745. This shared history is evident in the iconic red, white, and sometimes blue barber's pole that's still in operation today. There are many theories as to what the colours and pole represent, on of those suggest the red supposedly symbolises blood, the white denotes the bandages used. While the blue has had many suggestions of representation – from the client's veins to the patriotic completion of the red, white, and blue American flag.

End of the 19th Century

The end of the 19th century marked a huge change in the profession thanks to the creation of the very first barbering school. Established by A. B. Moler in in Chicago 1893, students were taught how to cut, shave, and give facial treatments. His institution proved to be such a success that others opened in nearly every city across America, and eventually across the globe.

The 20th Century

Into the 20th century and the barbershop had continued to be an important place for men to gather. A trip to the barbershop was usually a weekly occurrence. Opinions were discussed, games were played, and relationships built. Shops in this time appeared similar to the traditional barbers of today, with opulent surroundings and comfortable furnishings.

This was all to change in the 1920's thanks to the popularisation of the 'bob' haircut. Such a sharp and precise style could only be completed by barbers, and so shops had a huge influx of women clients. It has been suggested that up to 2000 heads per day were being 'bobbed' in New York City during this period.

From the 1920's onwards the profession evolved a great deal. There was a time where it seemed the institution declining, with men opting to visit hair salons or to avoid grooming altogether. Then came the 'barber boom'; a resurgence in the industry the likes of which has never been seen before and the very reason I'm writing this book.

Here in Britain we have an extremely rich history in barbering – including the iconic Pall Mall Barbers who celebrated their 120th birthday last year, and the oldest surviving barbershop in the world (Truefitt and Hill in London), established in 1805. London is also home to The Worshipful Company of Barbers, one of the oldest livery companies in the City of London, having celebrated its 700th anniversary in 2008. Nowadays this group is a fraternal organisation which provides support to charities, institutions, and individuals associated with the Company's ancient traditions and origins.

There are many reasons for the rise in barbering, which are hopefully going to be fully explored in the coming interviews. Social media has been a big part of the global popularisation, as has the general appreciation and growing trend of male grooming. Rather than visit unisex salons men are choosing to visit barbershops again, creating a demand that has revitalised the field. Thanks to this more money has been invested into products, tools, and education. We can only hope this continues long into the future and I feel that this is only the beginning. If we as barbers continue to grow and expand our knowledge and skill set, not only will our clients benefit, but so will we. As our skills grow, new tools, publications and opportunities arise, you just have to take a look at the progress in the last 5 years to see that this is true. This has me incredibly excited about the industry's future which is in all of our hands, let's take it further than we thought possible.

My Journey

I entered the hair industry almost 15 years ago, volunteering on Saturdays for the last few months of my A levels at my local TONI&GUY after my mother suggested this as a career option, due to my lack of interest in university. This got my foot in the door and led to my acceptance onto an apprenticeship which began in 2002. To my surprise it was a perfect fit and the ball started rolling. My career really began picking up speed when I opened my first salon 5 years ago, encouraged by my parents who were a driving force in this decision, and in the inception of the business and beyond. The timing was finally right for me – I'd previously been focused on my music, but now I was ready to buckle down and was motivated to succeed in the barbering business. It was incredibly difficult to leave my previous employers having spent years perfecting my craft there, but I longed for the creative freedom opening my own salon would offer. I needed to take the next step. When it came to my shop, I poured my heart and soul into its creation. I wanted a unique, innovative and stylish salon which mirrored who I wanted to be as a barber. I feel that we got it right, even though it was a little forward thinking for the sleepy seaside town of Torquay. Especially when we opened the doors and people asked questions like 'So you had to open before you were finished?' about the exposed brickwork and 'When are you going to put carpet down?' about the wood floor. Seriously though, can you imagine carpet in a barbershop?

It wasn't long before it started to pay off. By chance I met the amazing photographer Rob Grist and produced a couple of hair shoots. This led me to being contacted by Grant Northover, owner of Phab Wholesale (a leading distributor of hair products based in the South West and provider of educational courses) who asked me if I would be interested in becoming an educator. He asked me what my 'thing' was when it came to hairdressing as he wanted me to teach a course on that. I was completely flattered but also stunned – the thought of educating people was terrifying! That being said, I'm a firm believer in saying yes to every opportunity. It's better to regret the things you've done rather than the opportunities you've missed. I pondered over what my 'thing' actually was? What did I feel passionately about? The answer was obvious really: men's hair.

I had always had an interest in this area of hairdressing, this was my niche. At TONI&GUY no clippers were allowed, only scissors and a comb, but that didn't deter me. Although using scissors over combs is an incredible discipline and a fantastic skill to have, I had such an enthusiasm for alternative hairstyles that I went and bought some Wahl Super Tapers. To create mohawks and other alternative styles there was no competition to a set of clippers, so armed and ready I taught myself barbering on friends after work hours in the kitchen of my flat at the time. I was lucky to have the friends willing to donate their hair to learning. My colleagues chose not to pursue this avenue at the time, but for me it was a creative and exciting outlet which led to a large amount of men walking through the door and sitting in my chair. Especially as the rest of the team would send every guy that walked through the door or called to book in my direction.

After speaking with Grant the date was set for my teaching debut in men's hair. I was petrified but no matter how much an imposter I felt, I refused to disappoint Grant. I was such a wreck I had my first and only panic attack just days before the course was scheduled. I was cutting a friend's hair and explaining to him about how I had set up another trial day with the students of South Devon College to try and prepare myself and steady my nerves. This is when it hit me and I had no idea what was going on at the time but I had to step away and thankfully my now beautiful wife Tenneille had to step in and finish the cut for me. At that point I nearly threw in the towel but at the back of my head all I could think was 'I can't let Grant down', so I spoke to my parents and told them how I felt. They informed me that of course I didn't have to do it if I didn't want to, yet there might not be another opportunity if I let this one pass. Incredibly true and sound advice. I decided I wasn't going to let this chance slip past. I got through the trial with South Devon College, although extremely nervous and incredibly terrified when I stepped into that room full of students all sat waiting for me. It was the first time Id really felt this kind of pressure but by the time Id finished the first haircut demonstration I was far more at ease. With the support of my family and their belief in me alongside a successful trial run, I knew I'd get through the big day at Phab Wholesale and Education.

When the day finally came I was incredibly nervous but it went better than I could've ever imagined. I was booked a further 4 times in that year alone, with each course being completely sold out. I'm now a regular educator at Phab and teach in salons and colleges too – something I never thought possible. I also have Grant to thank for providing the platform which led to the confidence that then allowed me to be able to demonstrate my creations through platform work. This included being part of the talented True Beauty team for Keune in Amsterdam in front of 2000 hairdressers from over 70 countries, still the biggest show I have been a part of to date and demonstrating at the B-Groomed event in Chicago. Grant gave me this opportunity without knowing if I would fail or succeed and I'm eternally grateful for his trust and belief in me.

As I continued to work with Rob Grist I found myself gaining more confidence in myself and my ability to create. I'd finally found my niche and had a clear direction in my career, so I decided to enter a competition. We managed to reach the finals of American Crew's Face Off competition with 3 of our entries. I couldn't have been prouder and pleased at the time. The whole experience was hugely positive and led me to realising another dream of mine: to compete in the Wahl British Barber of the Year Competition on stage at Salon International. I've attended this event since my career began and always dreamt of gracing one of the stages at the largest industry gathering of the year, so I couldn't be happier. The fact that it was the Wahl stage alongside two of my great friends in the industry, Davie Walker and Paul Mac made it all the better.

Rob and I put together the #Th13teen Collection to celebrate my 13th year of hairstyling, as well as to promote education with Phab. This documented a group of men's hairstyles I'd designed, and was the very first time we got published, and it was in the prestigious *Modern Barber Magazine*. I can't thank Rachel Gould enough for that honour. The collection was a huge project and very ambitious. The fact we shot 13 models over the period of 3 days, in 3 different locations is still such an achievement to me. Looking back this hard work and the hours it took created success that became life-changing in that moment as it paved the way to being featured in other publications, including *Hairdressers Journal, Barber NV, Professional Barber*, and magazines in Brazil and the USA.

As the last 5 years have passed by I've continued to creatively and professionally challenge myself. This – paired with the growth in the industry – has given me so many opportunities. I've been able to travel, test products and tools, become a brand consultant, demonstrate my work, teach, learn, be published globally, organise events, be on television and radio, and make some great friends at the same time.

One of the things I'm most proud of in my career is founding The Lions Barber Collective, a charity that raises awareness of mental health issues with a focus on suicide prevention. The concept came from a single comment on Facebook and then developed fast because as a barber we have a unique relationship of trust and intimacy with our client. We are also currently working on implementing BarberTalk – a training program to help barbers across the nation and world recognise, talk, listen and signpost. We also hold Lion's Den events monthly (where anyone can drop in and speak to a mental health professional) which is open to any barbershop to join up to, as well as raising awareness though our walks and blogs. It's a cause that's extremely important to me, and my hope one day is for our BarberTalk mental health training to be implemented into all barber qualifications which would make a huge impact.

The most important thing I've learnt is nobody gets to the top or gains success without help from others. My journey would've been completely different without my family, friends, and the Tom Chapman Hair Design team. My parents and wife have unending amounts of patience and do all they can to support me. This industry has also been amazing to me since I opened the doors to Tom Chapman Hair Design in 2011 right through to making the decision to sell the shop in 2017, allowing me more time to focus on travel, education, The Lions Barber Collective, writing, and many other projects I now have the time to explore. There have been several people who've given me breaks along the way, and I couldn't have found this success without them. To those people (you know who you are) I'm still thankful to this day. Without them none of what I've done would've been possible.

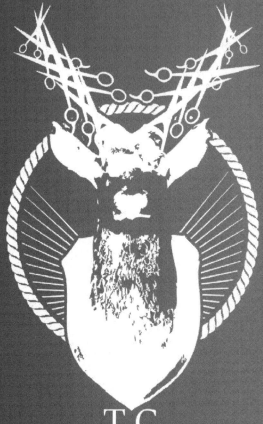

TC
Interviews

Chapter 1

Dan Davies

General Manager of Pall Mall Barbers

I met Dan at the Chicago B-Groomed event, and after spending many hours in his company I eventually found the right time to sit down with him for my very first interview. It seemed appropriate for Dan to begin this book; he's a passionate, talented, and well-respected member of the profession. He's also the general manager of the renowned Pall Mall Barber who have played a significant part in the renaissance of this industry.

Dan places great emphasis on education (evidenced by his role as advisor and assessor of City & Guilds), works in conjunction with well-known international companies (including MasterCard and WWE), writes for publications, and is a great giver of advice. It only seemed fitting that he kick off this journey.

Backstory

"I've been in the hair industry since 2001 – a 15 year rollercoaster of ups and downs. I started as a hairdressing apprentice at Ragdale Hall after my career as an aircraft engineer in the Royal Navy didn't quite go as planned, due to the fact I was rubbish at mechanics. So what does a clueless 19 year old lad do? I spoke to my granddad of course. He said get a trade and I couldn't go wrong. So that's exactly what I did.

The one thing that motivated me more than anything else was ladies – I was a 19 year old lad after all! Near my hometown of Melton Mowbray there was a massive health spa called Ragdale Hall advertising for hairdressing apprentices. There were 100s of women working there, so I thought why not give hairdressing a go? If I was no good I'd at least have the chance to meet some new people. A few good friends of mine were in the trade and helped me out with kit and getting my head around the basics. My 2 year apprenticeship had some highs and lows. I met amazing people (some of whom I'm still close friends with to this day), was employee of the month, and developed my customer service skills immeasurably. This initial experience was essential to my personal and professional development.

After Ragdale a friend suggested I join a small salon called Sharps in Melton Mowbray. This was the kick start I needed. I worked for 6 months at Sharps but wanted to learn more. A good friend of mine, Kev Hubbard, said there was a job opportunity at the barbershop he once worked at. The standard of this shop was high and it was a great opportunity to learn, develop, and have an increased income. I got myself the job at Males Barbershop and soon realised barbering was a lot more difficult than hairdressing! There was zero room for error, and what I was previously taught about men's hair was complete crap. I had to step up quickly or I was going to be without a job. Thanks to 2 amazing peers, Pat and Claire, I was able to learn some important tricks and skills. I'm so grateful to them, as well to as my understanding friends who let me try out my new techniques and perfect my skills.

I went on to stay with Males for 8 years and it was great. I was the man about town, I felt famous. I would go out and everyone would say hello and I'd never be without a drink. It was whilst still at Males I went on holiday with a couple of pals to Gran Canaria. There I fell in love at first sight with my now wife. The one downside to this was that my wife was not from Melton Mowbray. When I showed her the town she really wasn't keen on the place or the famous pork pie. So I made the incredibly tough decision to move down to Surrey. My work family and friends were massively supportive, making the transition easier.

I had 2 interviews where I really liked the feel of the places: Headcase and Jacks of London. I chose Jacks. After 2 weeks had gone by I knew I had made the wrong decision. The service seemed rushed as all of the pay was on commission. My ego was too big to go and ask Headcase for a chance (a decision I regret) so I went to work at a local barbershop in Weybridge called Harveys. I liked Harveys, it reminded me of Males and my barbering was the strongest in the shop. Everything was going great until I took the weekend off and the owner of the shop Facebook messaged me to say that he couldn't afford to keep me on. I found this quite a shock as I was massively requested by clients.

I went to work at few more locations around Walton on Thames all with zero job satisfaction. At one place the owner and his brother were talented beyond belief, but were arrogant and believed they were the best barbers that'd ever lived. Demanding high standards in dress code and work but not showing any of these ethics themselves, they chose to smoke in the back room instead of looking after customers. They would gamble away takings (and often my wages) at the bookies. It was at this point I knew that if I wanted to fulfil my potential I needed to work in London to find a reputable shop.

My wife helped me write a CV and I googled the top shops in London. I had a few interviews but was really taken by a chap called Richard Marshall – the owner of Pall Mall Barbers. He needed a good barber to come in and make his mark. This was the opportunity I'd been looking for and I craved the chance to show them what I could do. Pall Mall Barbers was quite a bit different then; there were 6 chairs and the shop had only just started to open Saturdays. It would be a hard slog to gain and keep clients as all of the barbers bar one had 10 years' experience on me and were exceptional. If I was going to make my mark and develop, I needed to give something more. I made sure my section was the cleanest and talked to all the clients and make sure that if I didn't cut their hair they still knew who I was, so when people had time off they felt comfortable with me. This worked and soon I had a very busy book.

At the time I also had a note book in which I'd write ideas and training advice in. I'd give these to Richard which led to him giving me the opportunity to go into training, development, and management. 6 years on and Pall Mall Barbers now has 4 busy shops with a team of over 30 amazing barbers that I look after, as well as doing some amazing pop ups for some of the biggest brands in the world."

The 'Barber Boom

"When I first starting barbering it wasn't seen as cool or high profile. Men thought they were always better off going to a salon to get a haircut. This changed when guys wanted to get their hair really short on the back and sides. Salons took male clients for granted and barbershops capitalised, regaining clientele and providing them with sharp cuts. But how long will it last? Well I can see a few places doing really well, but in general I think the industry is letting itself down. Training needs to be stronger. Training providers need stronger regulations. In my opinion there are people within the industry that could've made a real difference, but instead of doing the right thing with their relevant organisations they chose to be greedy and promote themselves for their own financial gain. Everyone's fade game seems to be strong but what happens when clients don't want skin fades anymore? If the barbers can't provide great haircuts using razor and scissor techniques, men will soon scoot back to hair salons and forget all about their barber. I'm greatly concerned about the amount of business people jumping on the barbering bandwagon hoping to make a few quid, and am very grateful to be part of a company owned and ran by barbers.

I have some great friends in the industry and am always available to anyone who wants advice. I'm a man of principles, and as long as I can improve the standard of education within barbering and give everyone that works within Pall Mall Barbers the opportunity to better themselves, that's cool with me. The aim for any barber involved in the industry should be to make the barbers and students they train better than themselves."

Healthy Competition

"I stopped entering competitions because in my opinion the winners weren't based on skill. Sometimes it can be down to how marketable the winner is, where they work, what products they sell, social media outreach etc. The best title I've ever received is Daddy. I couldn't care less about barbering titles really. I'm happy for my friends when they do well in competitions, but in reality does it feed your family?

I do feel competitions are great for aspiring people looking for a new experience. I really like student competitions and will always help City & Guilds or any collage/barber school with their projects and competitions. There are so many 'barber of the year' competitions now, it's almost like boxing with all the different organisations. It all depends on what you want out of your career I suppose. I like doing demonstrations at shows, but in regards to doing competitions it's not really for me."

Products, Tools, Publications, & Events

"There's a lot more choice now for tools and products. I personally prefer Andis clippers and trimmers over others as I feel they cut cleanly and give a perfect finish. My best tool is the Andis T outliners, I love them. For me they're the best trimmers ever invented – really ergonomic. I also love the new ERGO hairdryer. It's quiet so it's great for doing demos as you don't have to shout over the top of it and it performs magnificently. My favourite product is the Pall Mall Barbers Sandalwood and Clove Cooling Lotion. My skin's really sensitive and this product has saved my bacon when I'm being used as a model for barbers learning to shave.

That being said, even within the best product ranges I don't feel any of them are complete. Every range has a few stand out products, only to be watered down by other items that have had little thought go into them. I was extremely proud to be part of the team that developed the Pall Mall Barbers Shaving Range. We decided the products available weren't good enough for the luxury wet shaves we provided, so spent 5 years developing our own.

Publication wise, I like anything that Pall Mall or I feature in! There are so many ace magazines: *Barber NV, Salon NV, Good Salon Guide, Modern Barber, Salon Evo…* It's great to have so many great publications involved in the industry and I'm happy to work with all of them.

In term of events, Pall Mall Barbers do some amazing pop-ups. I organised a pop-up barber event on behalf of MasterCard for the Champions League final in Milan. I took an epic team of professionals out there. It was sensationally hot and there were 1000s of people but we rolled up our sleeves and did some serious barbering, which led to us delivering a pop up again the following year in Cardiff. This has led to working with the NBA and follow-on work with UEFA. In terms of industry events, I always enjoy Master Barber Live and Salon international.

The Power of Social Media

"Do I use it...sort of...I prefer to save my accounts for being social and stupid with my friends. I feel social media has become such an important part of people's lives now, they feel they have to post everything on their walls. I find that a bit sad in all honesty.

Pall Mall Barbers uses social media well and has a great following, but in terms of putting pictures of haircuts I've done, that's not really for me. I'm using social media at the moment to try and gage interest for my new podcast for barbers, porKchop, and that seems to be going well. Though people are often disappointed when they look into my personal Instagram and instead of seeing haircuts they see me riding in a Sinclair C5."

Any Advice?

"For those new to the industry you've got to stick at it. Hard work pays off. I'm proof of that. There are going to be people who try and rip you off and stab you in the back during your career; use these experiences to make you a stronger person and a better barber. The best lessons I learnt were from the places that knocked me down. Also never be afraid to ask for help – we all need it. I still often need it. Some people have different skill sets than others so help them and then when it comes to it, they'll be willing to help you"

@davies_barber

Dan mentions the products game as something many barbers and companies have jumped on. Most of these self-named products are actually bought from chemists that have generic 'gels' and 'waxes'. Once you've chosen the products you want, a packaging and label design will be chosen. This means clients pay premium prices for 'signature' products which the barber in question had no hand in creating. That's exactly why I respect Dan and his team so much for developing their range over such a long period of time. It's a labour of love and will ensure you create a better experience for both those in the chair and those using the products.

Listening to Dan speak about his career path, it seems there could've been a few times when he could've given up on barbering altogether. It's his drive and desire to succeed that led him forwards, and by committing himself to perfection once he landed his job with Pall Mall Barbers he has established one of the best networks in the profession today. Networking is so important in any walk of life. Remember it's not just who you know, but who knows you. It's no good just having them on your Facebook friends list. If you cannot contact them, ask their advice or a favour and get a reply, then they are not in your network. The same works both ways also.

T C

Interviews

Chapter 2

Jonathan Tayloni

CEO - El Patron

The next interview was with Jonathan Tayloni – owner and creator of Chicago-based grooming range, El Patron. I met Jonathan in Chicago at the first ever B-Groomed event and he told me all about his brand and said he'd love to work together. Since then I've been lucky enough to complete educational videos and classes with him, as well as visit both Nevada and California providing education for his brand. Jonathan has been in the industry for most of his life, so I thought he would be a great choice for a second interview.

Backstory

"I grew up in the business. My father was in the beauty industry and my grandfather too. From the time I could understand where I was, I was already a part of it.

I started at the age of 5 accompanying my father on global business trips and learning all about the importance of hard work and determination. After school I worked for various pharmaceutical companies, learning corporate structure. 5 years later I came back into the business and began implementing my newfound knowledge. I spent a season calling on salons and barbershops and through this research I learned a lot about the professional industry. I went door to door selling products and communicating with stylists and barbers to help me understand their needs, wants, and demands. The professional channel was unanimously calling for a true men's line. Stronger hold, better performance, retail and man friendly. This is what led to the creation of El Patron

I'm lucky enough to have worked on both sides of the industry, and have been honoured to be the recipient of 2 awards in my career. I don't take full credit for either, as teamwork is everything."

The 'Barber Boom'

"Within barbering I see the strong getting stronger and the weak getting weeded out. I see the return of the gentleman; a modern man who cares about fashion and lifestyle. This will circle back fully to barbers being the connoisseurs of style, with the barbershop replacing the long gone social clubs. I see more middle class men turning to barbershops as a place to socialise, leading to more lounge-type barbershops and turning more barbers into business men."

Healthy Competition

"People tend to love competitions, it's the closest relation to sport we have and is treated as such. It's also a good way of substantiating one's career, especially in this world of global communication. The inevitable evolution of social media makes it unavoidable. I actually evaded it for a long time, but it appears to be the best way of communicating your skill and style to the world.

Products, Tools, Publications, & Events

"Products and tools are our vehicles to get us where we want to be. They help us look and feel good, make livelihoods, and help unite us. This has always been the nature of man, to make things that better our lifestyles and overall wellbeing. Hopefully the brand of El Patron (and myself) will be a positive influence and leader in this field.

When it comes to my favourite product, it has to be our El Patron Aloe Vera and Eucalyptus Shampoo which helps heal and prevent damaged hair. I've worked with my own chemists to develop this shampoo so know exactly what goes into it. My favourite publication is *Master Barber Magazine*. We've worked with them on a few occasions to great avail. My favourite event has to be Cosmoprof Italy."

The Power of Social Media

"There are many benefits to social media. The most important in my view is the ability to get your message out to a huge amount of people around the world and being able to connect with like-minded people – either within or outside the industry. It's been a great tool for my brand and continues to serve it well."

Any Advice?

"My advice to anyone would be to do what you're passionate about; you'll enjoy every day and it will lead to infinite opportunities!"

@elpatronusa

Within these first 2 interviews I was already beginning to see some valid but opposing ideas. Jonathan appreciates the value of competitions and of social media, whereas Dan has conflicting views. It goes to show that everyone has their own approach to success. Drive is the one thing that unites them, and it's integral to any occupation. I was very intrigued by Jonathan's vision of the return to the gentleman, and it's something I've seen in the industry myself, and in the presentation of masculinity as a whole. Men are really starting to take care of themselves more and more, and although this could be because of social pressures in today's society, I like to believe that most guys are doing this for themselves. Men are taking more care in their appearance in the media and beyond, and that can only be a good thing for us as barbers.

Jonathan's advice made me consider the importance of passion in a career. Not everyone can achieve success in the field they feel most strongly about. I for instance happen to be incredibly lucky because I love what I do, but I didn't necessarily feel passionate about hair before I started out. If you don't enjoy something and feel stressed just thinking about doing it, then maybe it's not for you. Take some time to really think about your interests and then take action. If it's a complete change in direction with your job that will affect you financially, that needs to be considered. In "The 5 Second Rule" by Mel Robbins, she suggests to take up your passion as a hobby first, alongside your current job. This means there's no financial pressure on you which could stop your new career before it even starts.

T C

Interviews

Chapter 3

Andrea Lynne Raymond

Founder of The Asylum Barbershop &
Wahl Artistic Team Member

After 2 informative interviews with experienced industry leaders I wanted to get a different perspective – one of a relative newcomer. Andrea Lynne Raymond has hit the floor running in the past few years, competing against some of the most talented names around and claiming one of the most coveted titles in barbering.. I was excited to pick the brain of such an ambitious and gifted professional.

Backstory

"I've been barbering since April 2013 and have been lucky enough to have had a very successful start to my career. This included wining the prestigious Wahl British and Irish Barber of the Year in 2016.

I finished school in 2012 and went straight into women's hair. After a year I wanted to do something a little more challenging, and what presents more of a challenge than the precision of barbering? So I took a barbering course by night at the fantastic Bladez Barbers in Cork. I didn't think I'd like a career as a full time barber and was a little unsure going into it, but I think like most people I instantly fell in love! I started as a junior barber and worked my way up at Bladez until 2015 when I moved to Lancaster Barbers. I've been here ever since and now run an academy one night a week.

As of now I'm not as recognised as I'd like to be. I represent lady barbers, and with the platform I gained this year I hope to build on that. I'm ready to push more females to get their names out. Being the first Irish competitor to win the Wahl title, I'm hoping to help the Irish barbering scene to break through too."

The 'Barber Boom'

"I haven't been barbering for long but in the last year the industry has become huge! It's now cool to be a barber and people are recognising it as a serious profession. Barbers have started to up their game and take more pride in their work, which is a great thing for everyone."

Healthy Competition

"I think they're great, not just to get yourself recognised but also because it teaches you a lot. It gives you a great confidence boost – provided you get involved in the right ones. I don't think there's a particular barber that's 'the best'. There are a handful of barbers who all have strong points. I like to think we all have the same potential, but we're at different points of our careers."

Products, Tools, Publication, & Events

"I think there are a lot of products out there, maybe too many. Everyone is trying to have a go at making their own brand. It's the same with the huge range of clippers, shears, combs, and brushes available. It's great because there's a variety of haircuts and styles out there, so it's nice to have the right tools for the job – it can make all the difference.

My favourite product at the moment has to be any boost or volume powder – they're so diverse! They can be worked into any style or haircut, creating a number of different effects. Wahl's Finale Foil Shaver has to be my favourite tool. It's amazing for finishing off any haircut from a ghost skin fade to a tight beard line up – even those extra hairs around the ears. I often use it for scissors trims and to sharpen up the hairline, providing the client with a really clean finish.

Out of all events I've been to, the most impressive has to be Salon International at ExCel in London. It has a huge set up, full of demos, stands, and sales. There's so much to learn about every aspect of the hair industry, as well as both large and up-and-coming brands."

The Power of Social Media

"I use Instagram, Facebook, Twitter and Snapchat. Social media has a huge role in modern barbering for advertising, staying in touch with events, and keeping up to date with styles. I find Instagram a great place to go to get inspiration"

Any Advice?

"My advice to any barbers, aspiring or otherwise, is stick to your own style. Don't try to be like anyone else and you'll stand out. Also to lady barbers, push yourself. We can do just as well as any male barber, so long as we have the right attitude."

@andrea_lynne_hair

I really enjoyed listening to Andrea's perspective as a young, award-winning female barber, who occupies a mostly male environment. Although she's still relatively new to the industry, Andrea's story shows that seizing the right opportunities and having a positive attitude can make a huge difference in furthering your career quickly. Since this interview she has become part of the Wahl Academy team – an incredible achievement and something that not many people get the opportunity to be part of. It is an elite team, to say the least. As well as that Andrea has opened the doors to her very first barbershop, The Asylum in Cork City with Leanne Edwards. To say barbering was meant for Andrea may be an understatement.

You can springboard yourself into some fantastic positions through not only hard work and skill, but also being nice and exceeding expectations as Andrea has. You can be the best barber in the world but if you have a poor attitude and are lazy or confrontational, people won't want to work with you or recommend you for future opportunities. It's a lesson we as barbers should all learn.

TC

Interviews

Chapter 4

David Hildrew

CEO, The Bluebeards Revenge

My next interview was with the respected product owner of The Bluebeards Revenge and The Shaving Shack, David Hildrew. His story is fascinating and he has made such a success with both of his companies I knew he had to be a part of this book. I've worked alongside David and his team often, and have admired how they've grown in such a relatively short amount of time. There's no sign of this progress slowing down, as they are constantly developing new products and innovating ideas. His background is a polar opposite from Jonathon of El Patron who has been involved in the industry since birth, so I was intrigued to see how and if their opinions would differ.

Backstory

"I launched The Shaving Shack (a website dedicated to selling high-quality men's grooming products) in 2006. This endeavour gave me the inspiration to develop my own brand to sell all over the world. The Bluebeards Revenge officially launched in July of 2010 and has grown in strength every year, so much so it has picked up many respected awards – most notably *FHM* Grooming Brand of the Year and Best Shaving Cream Range at Barber Connect. In terms of recognition for the brand, I couldn't have asked for more. The Bluebeards Revenge has grown so much since we began, but I'm still the Bluebeard-in-Chief.

We're trying to become the number one barbershop brand not just in the UK but globally. We've dominated the domestic professional shaving sector for the past few years and now we want to make advances into the hair care/styling sector. We're developing a number of new products and hope to launch these very soon.

I'm not your typical brand owner. I haven't got any marketing education or degrees to my name. My background is a military one. I served as a Royal Marine in the Falklands and these experiences certainly shaped me as a person. The Bluebeards brand really reflects and captures my personality, even the packaging is still very much down to me."

The 'Barber Boom

"I'd say I started to see the resurgence around 5-6 years ago, and every year the industry goes from strength to strength. When I left the Royal Marines in 1988 my friends in the military were all looking to go into the building trade when they finished. Today squaddies want to become barbers. The trade is seen as cool and current – this means it's only going to get stronger.

I think the industry will continue to grow and standards will hopefully improve even further. Barbers need to continue to set new trends and develop new styles. A lot of hairdressers are now looking to either become barbers or adding barbering techniques to their skill set. The future of the industry is bright and hugely exciting."

Healthy Competition

"I love competitions as I'm highly competitive by nature. I also think they really help to promote the industry and raise standards. That being said I think there are too many 'barber of the year' competitions, which in turn makes it difficult to know which ones have kudos and prestige. The best barber is a very subjective question, but I enjoy the work of MK, Gareth Clark, Alan Jones, Tom Chapman, Liam Hamilton and Alan Beak."

Products, Tools, Publications, & Events

"The market for men's grooming has become very saturated over the past few years and we constantly have to innovate to stay ahead of the game. The standards of products (both hardware and consumable) have improved greatly. This has been helped by the improvements in technology, a better understanding of how products should work, and a focus on ingredients.

If I had to pick a favourite product, it would have to be The Bluebeards Revenge Shaving Cream. We launched it all those years ago and it still remains one of our bestsellers."

The Power of Social Media

"Social media is a great way to check out the work of barbers all around the world – and of course to market my own products. I leave this to my talented PR and marketing team who're on Facebook and Twitter all day. Even though I don't use these tools myself I fully understand their importance to the brand, and we wouldn't be where we are today without them."

Any Advice?

"Take the time to learn your trade properly and never think you've learnt it all. Talk to people who've been in the industry and listen to what they say. Get to as many trade shows as possible, watch the demos, and network. I'd also take the time to read industry magazines and connect with fellow barbers on social media. Enter competitions – and above all else, enjoy what you do."

David's journey is an especially interesting one in comparison with my previous interviews. He has no background in hair or marketing, yet he has achieved incredible success with both. There's no doubt his timing was perfect; he saw a gap in the market and ran with it. That being said it's not timing alone that creates success, if you have a good idea and work hard at it, you can accomplish a great deal no matter what.

Since the inception of The Bluebeards Revenge the 'barber boom' has exploded alongside the rise in the brand. It's now down to people like David and ourselves to read the direction of barbering in order to establish our businesses or careers, so once it peeks we can continue to evolve and ensure longevity. With their ongoing development and research into new products and tools I think they have a huge role to play moving forward and driving 'the barber boom'.

TC

Interviews

Chapter 5

Juan C Ramos

CEO, J. Ramos &
International Wahl Educator

After some fantastic insight into the opinions of one impressive brand owner in my native home, I travelled across the pond to speak to Juan C Ramos – an international ambassador, educator, and director of his own product range as well as a giant in the clipper world. He was also generous enough to give me several of his products to try and I fell in love with 'The Matte' in particular; a fantastic finishing product that creates pliable separation and texture without shine.

I met Juan in Chicago and spent some time getting to know him. He taught me a lot about the differences between the USA and Britain when it comes barbering – standardisation being one of them. Throughout the interview he gave me brilliant answers about both the field of barbering and his personal journey that led to where he is today.

Backstory

"I've been in the Industry 15 Years as of today. I'm licensed in multiple states in the fields of cosmetology and master barbering, as well as being an international educator and ambassador for Wahl. I'm currently based in Long Island, New York.

I started at the age of 15 in my mother's small hair salon that had 3 stations. I helped to sweep up hair and attend to her clients. On the down time I'd force my friends into letting me cut their hair. Little by little I started teaching myself to cut different textures. My mother saw something in me and wanted to send me to beauty school. I responded with "….beauty school?! No!" but went anyway.

I became licensed and at the age of 18 and expanded her small 3 station hair salon into 12 stations, hiring more staff members and training them in men's cuts. 2 years later a hair salon in the same town came up for sale. I went to look at it, negotiated, and purchased it – I didn't tell my mother until the day of the closing. I renovated the location to add more barbering and styling stations, hired new staff and trained old ones. After about 8 months of managing the 2nd location, I moved back to the first original shop where I started. At this point in time I was attending my clients and running both locations with help from my mother.

A year later I heard of another salon/barbershop for sale in a town 30 minutes away. So I did what I knew best…I went out and looked at the location, negotiated, and purchased. What I did in the 2nd location I applied to the 3rd. At this point running all 3 locations started to become very difficult. I needed someone I could trust with the business side, so I asked my father for help in supervising the shops. At the time he was a foreman for a multi-million-dollar company which he didn't want to leave. After another 10 conversations I finally convinced him to join the team. With his help things got much easier. After another 2 years, I decided to open a 4th location. I spent a year getting the new place running, and then once again went back to my original shop to keep attending to my clients. Within the next 4 years I was able to open 2 more.

During the following 4 years I convinced my brother and sister to attend hair school and said I'd train them to help me run the businesses. Opening the 6th location was topped off with some great news; I was selected as a member of Wahl's Education and Artistic Team. I've toured with Ice Cube and the cast of the new movie Barbershop 3: The Next Cut, and visited numerous countries as an educator on their behalf.

After traveling all over the country and internationally I noticed the lack of men's grooming products. That's when I decided to produce my very collection, J. Ramos. Today I spend my days traveling for Wahl, finding time to see my clients, and promoting my collection…all thanks to a pair of clippers, and my mother who forced me to go to beauty school – possibly the best move I ever made."

The 'Barber Boom'

"I noticed a rise in barbering about 5 years ago when being a barber became 'cool'. In 5 years I see barbering taken to another level. Barbering will be seen a truly skilled profession, on the same level as a doctor or a lawyer. The barbering world has so much to offer, including education, management of a shop (or multiple ones), and product creation. I see myself as a symbol to motivate others to become greater then what they think they can be"

Healthy Competition

"I think competitions are great. Competition is healthy because it always keeps everyone striving to become better then they currently are. However being the 'best barber' shouldn't matter because in this industry because as I see it, we're all the best"

Products, Tools, Events, & Publications

"I feel products and tools are getting more advanced. The types we use today are not the same as they were 10/15 years ago. Everything is evolving to better our industry. Ofcourse Wahl are industry leaders and I put everything into developing my signature wet line."

The Power of Social Media

"Social media has driven barbering forward. I currently use Facebook, Instagram, Snapchat and Twitter; but I'm a heavy fan of the first 2. There are benefits to all of them, it all depends on your purpose. It's great to promote yourself as a barber, your business, your brand, or even just to use as a display area for your cuts"

Any Advice?

"My advice to anyone in our industry is never give up. Consistency is key, and that will get you anywhere you want to be in life. Set your goals and crush each and every one of them. Do what you are doing because it's your passion, and not because it's a job or a way to make money. Worry about your passion and everything else comes right behind it, falling perfectly in place without you evening knowing...."

@official_j_ramos

As you can tell, Juan is a fantastically driven person who loves what he does. His story demonstrates how many different directions barbering can take you. The drive he celebrates is pertinent to not only those in the barbering profession, but from all walks of life. He's very focused on his objectives – setting goals is an important part of success, yet studies show that 97% of us choose not to. This might be through fear of failure, lack of options, or procrastination. Having goals can create clarity and provide you with a sense of achievement. I try to push myself to set daily, weekly, and annual goal. It can be tough until it becomes a habit. Committing to this has helped me immeasurably; things that seemed unobtainable a year ago are now completed or on the way. Take a minute to think about what you were doing 5 years ago, what you're doing now, and where you want to be in 5 years' time. Having direction and structure to how you spend you 168 hours each week makes a huge difference. We all have the same amount of time, it's how we spend it that matters.

TC

Interviews

Chapter 6

Eric Begg

Slicks Barbers &
Osmo Ambassador

Next I travel to Scotland to talk to one of the best up-and-coming barbers in the country, Eric Begg. Over the past 18 months he's gone from strength to strength and worked with some of the best companies around. After being friends with Eric for some time now, his notoriety is well-deserved. He's been part a part of the industry for a while and knows it inside out, so I knew he'd provide a fascinating interview.

Backstory

Backstory

"This will be my 11th year in the barbering industry – and what a year it's been. In the last 12 months I've been lucky enough to become ambassador for the Osmo product range along with my business partner Greg Forrest. This is something I'm really proud of. I'm looking forward to big things in 2017.

I currently own Slicks Barber Shop in Glasgow with Greg. We started the shop with just us 2 and have now built it up to a team of 9. We have plans to expand and hopefully take it to 12 soon. The rise of our shop has been nothing short of outstanding, but it's something we're still really grateful for and humbled by! We'll always look to take it to the next level and never stop working on the business to ensure progression. Besides the shop, everything else we do (The Barber Bash, magazine work, and shows) is a massive bonus. I'd like to think we are one of the leading barbers in Scotland and can inspire some young talent up here.

I started my journey in a barber shop in Glasgow. My mentor at the time was an old school, classic barber with 45 years' experience and 7 shops. I received a wealth of knowledge from all the employees across his shops, as well as a lot of business know-how from him. I consider myself lucky to have learnt so many techniques from loads of different barbers and stylists. This meant I took something from each person and added it to my own arsenal. I worked there for 4 years before I took a year out and traveled Australia where I learnt about their barbering culture. When I moved home, it was all about Slicks. I started the process whilst working for someone else for 3 years, so I took my time before opening my first business.

In 5 years' time I'd like to see Slicks grow into another shop and expand the brand as much as possible, as well as continuing to work with Osmo."

The 'Barber Boom'

"I've seen the rise in barbering happening over the last 4 years, mirroring the general interest in male fashion overall. Guys were starting to look after themselves, paying attention to the way they dressed. With a stylish look there was a need for a suitable hairstyle to match. I even started to see younger generations looking sharper, wanting to choose their own hairstyle rather than what their parents decide for them."

Healthy Competition

"When it comes to competitions, they're a great way to get noticed and get your shop out there, but being the best you can be is all that matters. If you're always looking to improve and further your career your customers appreciate it. To me that's all that matters."

Products, Tools, Publications, & Events

"When it comes to tools and products there's loads of variety at the moment. All I can say is it comes down to preference and what you're most comfortable using to achieve the looks you as a stylist create. At the moment my favourite tool has to be my Andis Slim Line Pro – you can zero gap the blade, it gives sharp hair lines, and running time on the battery is awesome. My favourite product is Osmo styling moose, it lets me create some real awesome shapes and it's a great all round pre-blow dry product. I think right now the work companies do behind closed doors to create new tools and products help us so much, but it's down to personal preference."

The Power of Social Media

"We use Facebook for our shop information and it's probably our best marketing tool to gain new custom and share our shop experience with Glasgow. It's also a great way to stay in touch with customers. We use Instagram to share our work, which is mainly to show our customers what's on trend in the shop at the moment. I use it to share ideas with barbers who we respect to see if we can improve in any capacity. We also use it for inspiration. I'd say social media is a must nowadays, but has to be used in a positive way."

Any Advice?

"My advice for any young up-and-coming barber would be to surround yourself with the best mentor and team you can. Always have a great positive attitude and look to better yourself in every capacity. A positive attitude is the key to success."

@eric_begg

Eric makes some interesting points about barber development, in that you can learn so much from those around you. Standardised education is important to the growth of the industry, but so is experience in a shop and with professionals who know the trade inside out. That's one of the reasons I always opt for apprenticeship students over college-only trained ones. You're a product of your environment, and being the right shop can mould you into a brilliant barber, as well as teaching you the right etiquette. Eric mentions how he was lucky enough to work with so many different barbers in the beginning of his career. I couldn't agree more with. Watching is one of the best ways to learn in this trade.

Reflecting on what Eric said with regards to social media, each platform is designed for different uses and maybe they've evolved that way without design, but it's so important to post the right thing in the right place. It's no good just posting everything on Instagram and then sharing it to Twitter and Facebook. I see

Instagram as an online portfolio which demonstrates to the outside world (whether that be potential customers or industry giants) what we do and what we're about. You should be able to tell by the last 4 pictures posted what that person does in my opinion.

If you want a professional profile then you need to keep it exactly that, as this will also enable you to create a bigger following. Other barbers will follow you because of you cuts and techniques, not necessarily due to your pet cat or what you just ate. Although you could use the Instagram story function for these types of media, as it tends to give more of an insight into people's lives and personalities. It's important to interact with those who message or comment on your profile as these interactions can create even more opportunities and form a strong connection with those who follow you.

TC

Interviews

Chapter 7

Mike Taylor

Founder of BBA,
Owner Mike Taylor Education

For my next interview I wanted to get the perspective on another fast-growing facet of the industry, education. Mike Taylor was the ideal candidate. He's well-celebrated not only for his talent as a barber, but also for his role as an educator and plays a big part in developing new barbers to a high standard.

Backstory

"My story....I started near on 27 years ago. Barbering was always the career I wanted, but back when I left school there weren't any barbering qualifications so I went to work in a hairdressing salon. Luckily the clientele was 60% male so it was a good start. It wasn't until after I qualified I found a job in a barbershop. That's when I really learnt my skill. I opened my first barbershop in Newbury at the age of 20, and now have 8 barbershops across Hampshire and Dorset. It was actually staffing issues that got me into teaching. I struggled to find decent barbers, so I got in touch with my local FE College and started teaching their barbering course. I've been teaching ever since.

In 2009 myself, Hannah Grigg, and Graham Satchwell launched the British Barbers' Association with the aim of giving barbers a voice. From this I've made friendships that will last a lifetime and worked with some truly inspirational people. I went to parliament with The Hair Council to change The Hairdressing Act (1964) to include barbers. Now barbers can become state registered in their own right. My latest venture has been launching the Great British Barbering Academy which runs barbering courses nationwide. I'm also really proud to be the first ever barber to be awarded Master Craftsman status by the Hairdressing Council – the only government backed trade association.

I tend to spend most of my time at my training academy in Poole, Dorset, where I train and assess NVQ Level 2 and 3 Barbering, as well as run other barbering short courses. It's a lot of work, but I always try to spend time working behind the chair at my barbershops in Bournemouth and Lymington. I see myself as a solid barber with a good reputation, and hope to be able to pass on my knowledge to future and existing barbers."

The 'Barber Boom'

"I guess I saw the barbering industry starting to slowly grow since the mid 90's but I didn't ever see it expanding to what it is now. Now it's cool to be a barber! We live in a world where looking good is everything – looking good for your age is the new rich. I can't see barbering still being this cool in 5 years but I can still see a massive growth in the male grooming market as a whole."

Healthy Competition

"Competitions are a great way to get yourself out there. I've had a massive involvement in some of the big barbering competitions in the UK – I even started the National Student Barber of the Year Competition to help get students on the right track and get recognised. Who do I think is 'the best'? We all are! If you're enjoying your job, looking after yourself and your family, and your clients like what you do then, I think it's fair to say you're one of the best."

Products, Tools, Publications, & Events

"When it comes to the development of tools and products I remember barbers working with a pair of Super Tapers, a comb, and a pair of scissors – that's it. I love all the tools and products around now and I think we need them. I love the way barbers show pride and spend money on their tools – I think it shows how important their career and their clients are to them.

When it comes to my favourites though that's a hard one, so let's list a few:

> ➢ Products – In my shop, I use and sell The Bluebeard's Revenge, Jack Dean, American Crew and Dapper Dan.

> ➢ Tools – The Wahl Detailers take a lot of beatings, but I also love my Oster 97 clippers.

➢ Publications – We didn't have these until a few years ago but now we have 3 amazing ones: *Modern Barber*, *Barber Evo* and *Barber NV* are all great.

➢ Events – Well I have a lot to do with Barber UK with The Bluebeard's Revenge and the boxing ring, but I also think Barber Connect rocks!"

The Power of Social Media

"Do I use social media? Yes I'm getting into it… I use Facebook and Instagram. I also have a Twitter account and am trying to figure out Snapchat. I'm a bit of a dinosaur but I'm slowly getting there."

Any Advice?

"Take your time, enjoy the ride, and never stop learning. You've picked an awesome trade – enjoy it."

@miketayloreducation

I see Mike as an inspirational figure in the barbering world. What he has managed to create is incredibly admirable and has helped countless people in their journey towards a successful career. He may be "a bit of a dinosaur" when it comes to social media, but at its heart barbering is still a business of community, interaction, and building lasting relationships. Mike clearly prioritises these characteristics, as proven by his desire to continue working in his shops no matter how busy he is. For Mike it's not about being the biggest name in barbering. He has crafted a career as an influencer and is always looking forward to the future of the industry. The life expectancy of the 'barber boom' declining is something not addressed in my previous interviews, and it's a possible outcome all of us should be aware of. Realistically it can't last forever and may never grow as dramatically as it has the last few years, but that's why we as professionals need to ensure we're doing the best we can and evolve with the market.

The internet has played and will continue to play a huge role in this. There's most definitely a divide between barbers who started before and after it. Traditional business no longer exists as it once did; now you can start a global business by yourself in your bedroom with a laptop very cheaply. You can have your products designed in India by someone you've never met, and then made in a factory in China. The internet has altered the barbering world through the encouragement of shared knowledge and possibility of long distance business relationships. Now barbers can be known all around the world. As a hair stylist from Torquay, Devon, I couldn't have imagined I'd have been touring the states 25 years ago. That being said, I believe successful barbering will forever be a shop-front business based on relationships. So although the internet has changed some aspects of barbering, some will thankfully never change.

T C

Interviews

Chapter 8

Aileen Nuñez

Education Manager, Great Clips Inc.

The next person I spoke to is held in very high regard in the industry and has occupied several impressive positions. She's kind, generous, and has always helped me without expecting anything in return. I see her as responsible for the rise in a certain clipper company in the UK, and she has achieved this in part by her incredible personable nature. Her name is Aileen Nuñez and here is her story.

Backstory

"I've been in the industry almost 20 years. As a child, Barbies were my first customers. My Barbies always had the best hair and makeup in my group of friends. Then I became bored of Barbies and moved onto real people. I started off doing hair and make-up on my mom and grandma at 8 years old. My junior and senior year of high school, my mom enrolled me in cosmetology. This meant when I graduated from high school, I was already licensed to cut hair. For my next move I chose Great Clips (a salon franchise) because my mom's friend owned one. It was a perfect fit because I loved specialising in haircuts and enjoyed the culture there.

From there I moved up the company ladder, applying for my first corporate position as a Training and Service Representative at 23 years old. In a nutshell, I was a consultant for franchisees and managers and conducted training for the Las Vegas and St. George markets. Between 2000 and 2011 I received 3 college degrees: Associates in Applied Science (Computer Info Systems), Bachelor's Degree in Management, and Master's Degree in Management, (Specialty in Leadership). These qualifications have helped me a huge amount.

My career was always on the up with Great Clips. I held 3 other corporate positions from 2005-2014: Training Specialist, Education Services Specialist, and National Education Services Specialist. I lived in Sacramento and Chicago, travelling all around the U.S. With all this experience I caught another business's eyes: Andis Company. They saw my profile on LinkedIn and asked if I'd interview for their International Education Manager position. I spent

2 and a half years with them. I learned lots from the perfect balance of beauty and barbering they're famed for, including how to run an education department, network with industry professionals, and how to adjust to other cultures when travelling internationally.

My heart has always been with Great Clips though. After I left in 2014 I cheered them on from afar, watching them make positive changes and become the billion dollar company they are today. I wanted to be part of a culture that set the standard high and help to take the company to the next level. An Education Services Manager position became open for the West Coast, Hawaii, Alaska, and West Canada. It required me to move to Southern California and I jumped at the chance. Living in such a great city and being responsible for these markets was a dream come true. Luckily the feeling was mutual and Great Clips wanted me back. Well, here I am 6 months later and loving it.

I'm known in the industry for my association with Andis Company. However, since leaving I'm seen as a resource or consultant for the beauty and barbering industry as a whole. I receive requests all the time, and I love to help others out with advice and connect them with the right people. Some of the connections I made with Andis have become real good friends of mine because we have the same values and intentions which is to work for the greater good of the industry."

The 'Barber Boom'

"The rise in barbering has been strong in the last 3 years – it's been amazing to watch for those who specialise in men's grooming. In the coming years I see continued growth with more education than ever before. It seems to have been strong in the UK for quite some time, but it's now rising in importance in the U.S too. It will not only be barbering techniques in demand, but also knowledge of how to run a successful barbershop."

Healthy Competition

"I think competitions are great. They serve their purpose, which is to give attention to talent and provide education. There are many talented barbers out there; in my eyes the best barber is passionate, talented, and willing to share their knowledge with no ego. Someone whose focus is to be the resource for others, not a celebrity. There are too many big egos in the industry recently – the goal to empower through education is lost due to this."

Products, Tools, Publications, & Events

"I love how clippers have evolved with the use of lithium ion batteries, giving you the option of a cord or cordless options. The competition between companies provides innovative tools to make a professional's jobs easier, increasing the value in what we do. At the moment my favourite tools are my Matakki Black Ninjas. They're sexy and create everything from clean lines to shattered outlines/interiors with ease.

When it comes to publications, it's hard to pick a favourite so it's a tie between 2. I'm a fan of these 2 because of the people involved in their creation: *Modern Barber* (Rachel Gould), *Barber NV* (Joanne Reid)"

The Power of Social Media

"I use social media in different ways. Facebook is used on a personal level for family and friends, however some fellow professionals have become like family to me. Twitter and Instagram are for quick updates as well as to bring light to brands I'm endorsing, and to provide advice and motivational quotes/insights. All 3 are beneficial for reaching a global audience and promoting brand awareness."

@aileen2711

I enjoyed Aileen's interview because she's able to view the industry in a more encompassing way, thanks to working on both sides of the Atlantic. Her journey reiterates the different paths you can take as a barber, exploring formal education and learning about the business and market as a whole.

Aileen's relationship with Great Clips is a sound lesson for anyone, leaving a job on good terms (especially in a business like ours) is essential. The fact that she went back to her old company could be seen by some as a step backwards, but Aileen knew it was the right choice for her and went on to be even more of a success after her return to Great Clips. She's a fantastic role model for anyone in any industry, and to top it all off she's more than happy to share her knowledge and opinions freely. Another lesson we can take from her journey is to always leave people with a positive impression; even her favourite publications are based on the people involved and her relationship with them. People often say "nice guys finish last", I strongly disagree with this and as we can see,mm thankfully that's not the case with Aileen.

TC
Interviews

Chapter 9

Erin Wentworth

Pall Mall Barbers
Shave Ambassador

My next interview is with one of the best shavers in the business, Erin Wentworth. Although she's English, I met her in the states where I witnessed a demonstration of her phenomenal shaving skills. Erin works alongside Dan Davies of Pall Mall Barbers, and as a team they educate on stage all over the world. As a woman in such a niche market, I was excited to see how she viewed the industry and what led her to where she is today.

Backstory

"I started out 14 years ago when I was hired as a receptionist at prominent barbers called Geo. F. Trumper in London. I immediately fell in love with the barbershop atmosphere – especially the traditional hot towel shave service. I would watch the barbers for hours.

After a while one of the barbers was dared to let me shave him. It took an hour and a half, but I got through it without one nick. Thanks to this a barber overseeing the whole thing decided to train me. I trained in lunchtimes, before and after work – whenever we could squeeze it in. I qualified under his watchful eye, going on to work in Trumpers for the next 8 years.

I then joined Pall Mall Barbers becoming their shave specialist. I moved through the ranks to run their flagship store, taking on the responsibility of the juniors and finally becoming the brand/shave ambassador I am now. I've been with Pall Mall Barbers for 5 years and in that time I've been voted best shave in London in *Timeout*, as well as in a Norwegian magazine. I've also been lucky enough to grace the cover of my favourite industry magazine *Modern Barber*.

I like to concentrate on my shop and the juniors under my care, ensuring they have sure footing and a strong training base. Pall Mall does a great job of promoting me within media and the industry as whole. With this heightened publicity I can only hope to inspire young girls in training to dig deep, work hard, and sharpen their skills to become a new face in a man's world."

The 'Barber Boom'

"I noticed a boom in barbering around 5-6 years ago. Men were leaving hair salons behind, returning to the barbershop for traditional services such as shaves and beard trimming. I believe the popularity of beards has had a huge impact on the rise of barbershops, and in turn on the amount of trainees applying for jobs. Hopefully the future will provide equal opportunities in an ever-growing industry, with strict training for our future colleagues."

Healthy Competition

"When it comes to 'best shave' titles, I personally don't take part in competitions as I get a greater satisfaction from positive client feedback. That being said, I do believe competitions are a great way for barbers to interact with each other and push for greatness, which will only better the field as a whole."

Products, Tools, Publications, & Events

"All of a barber's staple tools are integral to making the most of their creativity and talent; the product is the cherry on the cake. It helps to highlight and strengthen the final look. Every barber has a preference towards certain tools and products, so I say each to their own.

My favourite product has to be Pall Mall Barber's own range – especially the Cooling Gel. As a shave ambassador who specialises in facial hair, this product is really useful. It's great for all skin types and has incredibly gentle, soothing qualities. My Open Razor is my go-to tool – certainly the one I've definitely used the most!"

The Power of Social Media

"When it comes to the internet, all of my social media pages are connected to my personal life. Pall Mall does an amazing job at promoting all of their barbers and talent on social platforms, so I find it best to leave it to the professionals!"

Any Advice?

"Barbering is a great big family. We share our products, talent, training, and ideas with each other on a regular basis. It's an industry that's inclusive to all, and being part of it is the greatest privilege anyone can ask for. The best advice I can give to any aspiring barber is to pay attention to absolutely everything around you in the barbershop. Watch the haircuts and shaves – you'll learn techniques that courses don't teach. Take in the 'talk' of a shop. It will assist your customer service skills immeasurably, as well as educating you further on products and styling.

Finally...listen to your teacher or head barber. They'll pass on a set of skills to you to hone and make your own. If you listen well and apply yourself you may grant your head barber's hidden wish – that one day you'll surpass their knowledge, growing to be the best you can be and eventually passing that talent onto the next generation of barbers. At least that's my hope for all my juniors."

@bettybunn3

Erin's passion for her craft and attitude to the industry are valuable lessons for any prospective barber. She learnt her trade in every available moment, and has great respect for the culture of the shop and for all the teachers and barbers who helped her along the way. I always say to any aspiring barber that along with gaining their qualification, they should volunteer in a local shop. The experience is priceless and will often secure you a place on the team once qualified, or even before.

She's also brought up a valid point yet to be discussed; how the popularisation of beards has pushed a lot more customers through our doors. As an owner of a unisex salon, I know some hairstylists are not confident when it comes to beards – especially as it's something not taught in standard training. It's certainly an extra skill more stylists should explore.

Finally I really admire Erin's approach to the future of the industry, to be a good mentor to her students. This is the most important thing we as experienced barbers can do – pass on knowledge and in the hope of making the next generation even better.

TC

Interviews

Chapter 10

Paul Nicholson

Black Sheep Barbers

For my tenth interview I spent some time with Paul Nicholson, a former hairstylist whose decision to move into barbering led him to immigrate to Australia. This is a dream for a lot of young professionals and not all of them know that barbering can help achieve it, as the Australian government acceptance of visa from hair professionals.

Paul is also proud to be part of our work with The Lions Barber Collective. He's an avid supporter of raising awareness of suicide prevention and promoting mental wellbeing through barbershops in Melbourne.

Backstory

"I've worked in the hairdressing industry for 17 years, starting off in unisex and then moving into men's hair 4 years ago. In May 2015 I began focusing solely on barbering at the prestigious and award-winning Savills.

I started hairdressing a week after my 17th birthday, although I worked before that in a little old ladies' salon around the corner from my house in Doncaster. I instantly fell in love with salon life and spent 13 years as a unisex stylist. Although I've left the industry multiple times I always come back – sometimes a little rusty but consistently keen to get right back into it. You have to have love for this career, otherwise you're doing the customer an injustice.

I rekindled my passion for the industry after my recent move to Melbourne, Australia. The scene here is totally different and seems to be lacking the brotherhood we have in Europe. I'm not totally sure as the reason for this as yet.

I came to Australia as a backpacker in 2007 and fell in love with Melbourne. I couldn't settle until I came back. For barbers and hairdressers there's lots of opportunity to work here and there are always sponsorships available as there's a massive skill shortage. My big struggle was my age and that I was unable to work here legally on my previous visa. It was a bit touch and go for me, but if you're under 31 it's a much easier process. I now work for a general order barbers and have taken on a managerial role. If you know any barbers who want to come out here, I'm looking to build my team.

When it comes to my position in the industry a few months ago I'd have said I'm no significant part of it, but recently I've fallen madly in love with cutting again. I'd like to think in the near future, I'll have established myself in Australia and hopefully be able to come home and mix it up with some of the best. I'd eventually like to do something within education, or maybe even represent a brand I truly believe in. If and when I leave the industry I want to finish on a massive high."

The 'Barber Boom'

"I've noticed the rise of men-only salons since 2007. I saw modern barbering as we know it now appearing in 2012 with hot towel shaves becoming more of a feature. Notably I remember someone asking me for a fade and I was like "a what mate?". Until that point I'd been more of a mods 'n' rockers type of hairdresser, using mostly scissors. It's fair to say I've been on a steep learning curve in the last few years. I believe barbering will continue to grow in the near future. There's still a lot of territory I've only just caught onto.

In my opinion the Australian market is still primitive in comparison to the UK, as are other parts of Europe. However, with the various big dogs in the industry spreading their knowledge globally this won't be the case for much longer. It's an exciting time for those who want to grow within the field, all around the world."

Healthy Competition

"There's such a diverse range of talented barbers our there it would be unfair to single one out as the best. That being said, I'm a hairdresser at heart so really love what Andrew Does Hair is doing at the moment, educating barbers to educate their customers. I also love Menspire – they're killing it right now."

Products, Tools, Publications & Events

"When it comes to tools, my god they have changed! Once upon a time you'd have one set of clippers. Now you have 5 in your kit, 4 different types of scissors, and combs for everything.

Male grooming products and regimes have also changed dramatically. You had gel or wax when I began my career, now you have a full arsenal of products. It's a good thing. It installs massive faith that the barbering industry is here to stay. When barbershops faced their demise in the 70's, it was because barbers didn't cut long hair and men didn't use anything other than soap. These days' men are much more self-aware, buying beard oils, hair products, using hair-dryers, cleansing, and talking openly about the barbers they visit. This can only be a good thing for us.

When it comes down to products I use Kevin Murphy Freehold for pretty much everything: blow drying, styling, finishing… It's like my salad dressing! My scissors are the jewel in my crown – being a "tight" Yorkshireman I use them as a razor and for thinning. Never underestimate the power of a good pair of scissors."

The Power of Social Media

"I watch what everyone is doing – the day I don't learn something from someone will be the day I walk away. Social media is a great way to do this. If I hadn't been active online I wouldn't be here in Melbourne, living in the best city in the world. Instagram, Facebook, Twitter and Skype have all paved the way for barbers to travel and hook up all over the world. I wish when I was a young hairdresser I'd had the opportunity to get myself out there like the lads coming through the ranks now."

Any Advice?

"Never stop listening. No matter how good you think you are, there's always someone better. Drop the ego, respect the game, and the players in it."

@fight_in__th3dog

I really enjoyed my time with Paul. He has such a wide knowledge of the hair trade, is always looking to improve himself, and make some interesting points – especially in terms of social media. We barbers now have so many resources at our fingertips; we can follow, learn, and draw inspiration from all over the world. This book was made possible by this very tool.

Paul mentioned the demise of the barber through the 1970's due to most not being able to cut long hair. There's still a chance of this happening again, though education and communication is much stronger and there's a huge market associated with male grooming. If a trend towards longer hair grows, barbers will be encouraged to start honouring scissor skills and evolve with the times or get left behind.

With that said we are incredibly lucky to be alive now, just look at the resources we have in our hands. We can follow people all over the world, draw inspiration, and learn from them. With our smartphones alone have the capability to educate ourselves and find out any information we desire, previous generations didn't have the opportunities we have now. Gone are the days when you would have to move to the big smoke to gain exposure or opportunity, it is now available to everyone from their own barbershop or hometown, no matter how remote.

Just look at this book, I've contacted people in person, as well as over the phone and through the internet. Without the internet I wouldn't have known any of these barbers, let alone learn so much from them and have the pleasure to interview them. It's so important to draw inspiration (especially from our peers) which is now so much more accessible.

TC

Interviews

Chapter 11

Sam Wall

American Crew Elite & Freelance Stylist

After my trip down under it was time to return back to the UK in search of Sam Wall; and incredibly talented barber based in the North East. With just 6 years under his belt Sam has won great respect in the profession, holding several awards and participating in London Fashion Week. I wanted to speak to Sam because he has a proven track record in the competitive world and I wanted to discover how this has shaped him and his opinions about the industry. He is also a big part of the men's fashion world, giving him unique insight into that part of the industry.

Backstory

"I'm Sam Wall and I've been in the industry 6 years. I'm a member of American Crew Elite and a freelance stylist who has been lucky enough to win many awards in male grooming.

I started back when I was 22 as a hairdresser with the intention of combining my 2 passions: hair and travelling the world. I was fortunate enough to receive high-end training in Mayfair, London, and have continued to learn ever since. In terms of the future, I want to keep pushing myself and see how much of an influence I can become in this industry."

The 'Barber Boom'

"The rise in Barbering started to become obvious a few years back, but has really increased at fast rate recently. I believe it will continue to accelerate in the coming years with the right guidance.

I'd like to hope barbering will soon become more significant in the fashion industry. Hairdressing has always been a played a huge part of it, and barbering might just be there within the next 5 years. In order to ensure the profession continues to grow, we all need to raise the overall standard of our work and the value of what we do. No more cheap haircuts – we need to be proud of the service we offer to the public and bring it up to the same level as hairdressing."

Healthy Competition

"Competitions are so important, however being the 'best barber' and winning is not. The reason I find competitions vital is because they push you as an individual and give you a platform to showcase your work. As for winning and receiving awards, that doesn't matter to me. I enter them to try and improve my own skill set and performance. The only person I ever compete against is myself."

Products, Tools, Publications, & Events

"Products and tools are vital as they greatly contribute to the end result. With there being a much bigger market available to us now, we as professionals need to expand our knowledge on which tools or products will best help achieve each desired look.

Publication wise, I'm a big fan of *Creative HEAD Mag* and *HJ Men Magazine*. Another one that stands out is *Modern Barber*. This was the original barber magazine and has provided a platform to popularise the profession.

My favourite products are made by American Crew – their range is fantastic. The best accompaniment to them? My favourite tools: a hairdryer, and a brush. The amount of styles you can create from blow drying properly continues to amaze me."

The Power of Social Media

"I'm on Facebook, Instagram and Twitter. For me it's important to use social media for yourself and in the right way. It has to relate to your business, so it's irrelevant how many followers you have. It's quality rather than the quantity"

Any Advice?

"My advice for up-and-coming barbers would be to simply keep an open mind and learn every day. Grow as a barber, but also as a person as well. Be the best you can possibly be and don't do anything halfheartedly. Give it your all in anything you do."

@mrsamwall

Sam has high hopes for the industry, and his prediction that barbering will become a more recognised in the world of fashion has great credence. The lines are becoming blurred between barbering and hairdressing, and more professional barbers are having an active role and receiving credit within the fashion world. At the same time a lot of hairdressers are moving over to and specialising in men's hair. This is supported by global brands like L'Oréal and Keune releasing their own men's ranges and pushing male grooming. It all points to a healthy, creative growth within the profession, for at least the immediate future.

He also makes an important point about educating yourself on the tools and products available to you. In the past scissor skills were all that mattered, but now a barber needs to be an expert on a whole range of different elements which make up the profession. Finishing and styling are integral to the client's experience now.

Finally, I was fascinated by Sam's attitude to competition, especially as he has such an impressive track record. It mirrors a lot of what other interviewees have stated: competition is the chance to push yourself and showcase your work. It's not the winning; it's the experience and exposure. Failure seems to be a scary word and we're taught to avoid it, when actually it can help us to learn more than winning ever could. As Zig Ziglar said, "Failure is an event, not a person".

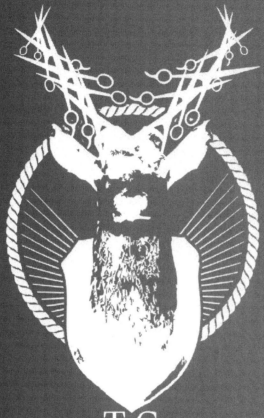

T C

Interviews

Chapter 12

Robert 'Bert'-Jan Rietveld

Co-Founder Reuzel & Schorem

This couldn't be a complete book about modern barbering without a trip to the Netherlands to speak with one of the most famous faces in the industry – Bert the Bloody Butcher. He and his business partner have revolutionised the industry with their own take on barbering in the form of their product company Reuzel and shop Schorem, achieving world-wide fame and professional success. Bert is a character who is unapologetically true to himself with bags of charisma – this combined with his expertise and love for the business meant I knew his interview would be a highlight and an opportunity I couldn't miss.

Backstory

"How long have I been hairdressing? Man, I started practicing my fades on bloody mammoths with a sabre tooth comb haha… I have to be honest my mind and memory are slightly hazy because of a certain way of living, but I'm pretty sure I did my first haircut when I was about 14/15 years old. I started f**king with me mates' hair… mohawks, psycho quiffs, that kinda thing.

During school I found I wasn't born to fit into the educational straightjacket. Back in those days they didn't have terms like ADD or ADHD, but I definitely had a big problem with authority and rules (still do). In high school I discovered I wanted to work with my hands, and through the skateboarding and music culture of the time I somehow ended up cutting hair at my parents place. Now don't get me wrong, I didn't know sh*t about hair. I just tried to copy record sleeves and stuff I saw in skate videos (this sounds way cooler then it was, check out the haircuts of Powell Peralta's Bones Brigade haha).

After screwing up a lot of hair and my education (they finally kicked me out) my mum sent me to beauty school. F**king hated it from day one, doing perms and finger waves. You gotta realise in those days there were no barber schools in the Netherlands. Luckily I found a job in a mixed salon where the owner was trained in classic barbering. He taught me all the basic techniques with an iron fist. Now I might have a problem with bosses and teachers that wanna force sh*t down my throat, but I'm very eager to learn when I'm interested in a subject. I'll read everything I can find and practice till my fingers bleed... Funny thing though, once I mastered men's hair he kinda pushed me into women's hair. That's when I really started learning. I fell in love with the philosophy and work of Vidal Sassoon, (real punks don't need leather jackets, he was a true rebel). I think it's the combination of those 2 completely different forms of treating the same product that gave me my way of working today... Don't hate... Appreciate then educate...

Did I ever dream that Schorem would be the success it is today? Never... I dream about booze and women haha! I guess we're doing pretty good but I can easily show you a1000 barbers on Instagram who do way better fades and cuts then us. Barbering is an ancient craft, we didn't reinvent it. We stole a lot from history, we stole a lot from other shops and from certain subcultures, we mixed it all together and we called it 'Schorem'. This word means 'thieves', 'rogues', 'scoundrels' or 'scumbags', which makes total sense after stealing so much sh*t haha... I thank the gods every morning because I love my life and job, but in the end it's just a barbershop.

This is gonna sound horribly arrogant but I really think we were lucky enough to open our shop at exactly the right time. Before opening our doors I think Leen (my business partner) and me spent about 2 years getting all the details right. We knew exactly what we wanted and the quest for what would become Schorem (also lovingly known as The Holy Ashtray) began around 2009. This meant looking for the right interior style, back bar, chairs, floor, furniture etc., but even more importantly researching the history of barbershops in general. The idea of returning to my cutting roots and having a shop had been in my head for quite a while. I spent hours and hours on the internet trying to find as much information as possible. I looked a lot into the American barbershop, which has always been our main motivation and inspiration, as well as barbering around the globe.

I soon discovered there weren't that many barbershops around, or if there were they didn't have a Facebook page. Looking back it was probably the latter. I think a lot of barbershops just didn't see the value of promoting their shop on the web at the time. When we started our Facebook page it exploded, and within a year and we got more and more friend requests from barbers around the world…From that point we just continued to grow to what we are today."

The 'Barber Boom'

"It's hard to say when the whole renaissance exploded. I can only throw out a big hooray. The barbershop is back and it's not gonna go away.

I think barbering and men's hairdressing are fusing again. I might be a bit of a purist but for me the barbershop is a place for the average Joe that just wants to look good, rather than a place to get his eyebrows done or his beard painted on… Now don't get me wrong, I totally understand if you want to offer your clients services they're asking for, and it's up to you as a shop owner to decide if you just want to stick to cuts and shaves or expand your business. It's just not for me.

The only thing you should really care about is your patron and why he wants to come to your shop. The thing I like the best about the barbering being back is that a guy can now choose whether he wants to go to the salon or barbershop. The other great thing about the 'barber boom' is that I've never seen the quality of men's hair being as high as it is today. I just love the fact that more and more kids are choosing to become barbers. It was a dying trade but man, we're an army now. I just hope that older barbers realise it's all about education."

Healthy Competition

"When it comes to titles and awards, I have too many to mention… I come from a very small village where I was known to be able to p*ss the furthest of all the boys – that must have been my first award. I ate it though…best lollipop ever haha.

First and foremost, I'm the Bloody Butcher which is the biggest reward of all. If you want to know all my official titles you should probably ask Leen, my staff, or my former lovers. I'm sure you'll find such beauties as "the laziest w**ker in the universe" (Leen)… "arrogant, grumpy old man" (the staff) or "he who cannot be named" (ex-lovers) haha… I don't care about titles and awards man, especially in our trade. It's not about being the best it's about *giving* your best. I started to cut hair to get my buddies laid, and that's pretty much what I still do only my clientele grew a lot bigger!

To be honest I don't like competitions at all, although I've judged a couple of them. It's just not my cup of tea and I sure as hell don't care who 'the best' is. For me barbering is and has always been about the patron and having fun doing haircuts. When I do a haircut I really, really like, I just want to chop his head off and hammer it to the wall! It's the same with seeing my colleagues work – I just really enjoy seeing a great cut. I think with handwork it's impossible to choose who the best is. Of course it's about skills but it's also a matter of personal taste. A barber should also be judged by the way they treat their client. For me it has never been just about hair – in competitions you don't get a point for making a client laugh out loud"

Products ,Tools, Events, & Publications

"A great friend once told me a good haircut doesn't come from a tin, and I've always said it's not the tool it's the hand that holds it. This pretty much sums up my philosophy about hair, hairdressing, and barbering. It doesn't matter if you're using a $10,000 pair of scissors and 8 different products, in the end it's always the quality of the haircut that matters. It should be the shape of the haircut that does the work – if you need product to make you hair look good, you just got a sh*tty haircut.

I see guys at events with tool cases the size of containers, whereas I've travelled the world with 2 combs, a vent brush and a WAHL Super Taper haha! I can get really jealous when I see barbers using 16 clippers doing a perfect fade, but it's just not my thing. I'm way too chaotic for that. I've always been a WAHL guy for the simple reason it's the first clipper I ever had and the one I was taught to use. I'm a creature of habit. It's very, very hard to make me change when it comes to tools or brands. Same with products. We have a huge collection of pomades from around the world, both big and small brands. I've tried them all but in the end I always go for a mix between a strong and a medium hold oil based product – in my case the pink and green Reuzel pomade.

The night we came up with the name 'Schorem' we got absolutely hammered and joked about making a product called Reuzel, which means lard in Dutch! We just thought it'd be hilarious if a guy was telling his friends he was using bacon fat to grease up his hair. When we opened the shop it was hard for us to find a company to buy our pomades from. A lot of it we had to order in the States and it got held at customs for weeks. With taxes we were selling these products for 3 times their price in the US, and clients sometimes had to wait for weeks to be able to buy them. That's when the whole Reuzel story came back to us. Being an old punk with a DIY ethos, I actually cooked up the first can of Reuzel in the kitchen of Schorem and almost set the whole place on fire! It took us about 26 months from that can to finally have the first tin in our hands.

There are a million stories to tell about Reuzel, but in short we were very lucky to meet the right people at the right time who helped us out. I think we've created one of the weirdest, most awesome brands out there by just following our gut. Everybody told us that putting a pig on a tin that easily dents (we did that on purpose, for us a can of grease should look a bit battered) and calling it lard was the worst idea in the world. Sometimes you just gotta stick to your beliefs. I still love the fact that it's a punk rock story, although it's hard to believe it grew into such a world-wide spread brand."

The Power of Social Media

"Man, it's weird... Schorem has a combined following of about 1.3 million people on Facebook, Instagram, YouTube, and Twitter. I'm sure it's social media that has brought us to where we are today.

The world has changed so much, now people in Hong Kong can look into your shop just as easy as your neighbour could. Before social media you just had the window of your shop and your haircuts on the street to spread the name of your business. You had to work hard to draw attention to yourself, maybe post an advertisement in your local newspaper. Now you can show the world what you're all about, but that can also be tricky.

Social media is like a hungry monster in your basement. The more you feed it, the hungrier it gets and the more it grows… you get the picture… As much as your online reputation is important, do not forget about your business. I know there are a lot of people out there that forget about their actual day job because they're too busy selling a dream on the internet. You may have 100,000 followers but they're not paying your rent. It's better to take care of the 20 clients that do. I used to be a social media junkie but I kinda took a step back from that, although we still do all of our marketing and social media ourselves."

Any Advice?

"Never forget the reason you wanted to become a barber in the first place – to take care of people and make 'em feel good about themselves. There's another 1000 good reasons, but this one should be on top of your list. Stay true to yourself and you'll find nothing is impossible. Hey if a f**k-up like myself can do it…."

@the_bloody_butcher

Both an entertaining and informative interview, Bert has raised so many points. Timing is a key concept that keeps cropping up for our barbers, but I think Bert would've been a success regardless. He believed in something, stayed true to his vision, and broke the mould – now his companies dictate trends around the world. An unexpected outcome that goes to show it's so, so vital to stick to your guns as a creative and be yourself. Bert also presents a version of the modern barber discussed in the opening of the book; someone who borrows from others in order to create something new. You don't need to reinvent the wheel, but you do need to do your research into what came before you.

He and Leen's punk rock approach to business melds perfectly with the growth of social media. At least for the moment, this tool lends itself to helping smaller businesses grow on a global scale. The culture of their shop is most definitely rock n'roll and is a perfect example of why barbering is seen as a 'cool' industry. Like other professional renaissances of late (tattooists for example) there's the outsider perception that it looks fairly easy and can be picked up in a short period of time. Like any other art, barbering take years to hone and success is built on skill, time, work, and little luck. Put in the hours, work hard, practice, never stop learning, and you stand a good chance. To observers looking in at someones achievements it can look like an overnight success, yet it took 15 years of hard work, dedication, commitment, chance, timing and connections to get to that point. Once there it can be equally as hard work just to stay at that level, hence why Bert and the rest of the Schorem and Reuzel team continue to improve and develop new skills and products.

TC

Interviews

Chapter 13

Farzad Salehi

Barber, International Educator
& Shave Expert

My journey now continued to Canada in hope of speaking to another shaving expert, Farzad Salehi. Known worldwide for his incredible shaving skills, I'd met the 'Happy Barber' (as he's known) in Sweden and have always found his work awe-inspiring. He really lives up to his name, being one of the friendliest in the business. Having the chance to not only speak to him again, but to also get his perspective for this study into our craft was an opportunity I couldn't miss.

Backstory

"Well if I count the 2 years of apprenticeship (the foundation of my career and one of the most important parts), it's almost 31 years. It's hard to believe it's been that long...it makes me feel like an old man! There was no separation between cutting hair and shaving in my time. When I began my apprenticeship whenever the boss cut hair I had to shampoo it, when he shaved I had to make the soap. That's how it began. It wasn't as if I just decided from childhood that I wanted to be a barber.....none of that. As with any profession (like carpentering, welding, or plumbing) you start from the bottom, learn skills, and make your way up.

Interestingly as far as shaving, I actually started doing more shaves after I opened my own shop here in Vancouver. I do more now and in recent years than ever before. Shaving is something I really enjoy doing, and I just found my own style of doing it that's comfortable and make sense to me. It also gives the client the most relaxing and enjoyable experience possible. For me this is the most important point about shaving.....how did the client feel?

I've proudly owned and operated my own barbershop in Vancouver, Canada, with my wife Shelley since 2006. It's a traditional, 2 chair shop that provides men's haircuts and straight razor shaves. We have one other barber, Noriko Matsuguchi, who's been with us for more than 9 years now. Shelley manages all aspects of the business.

Every day I'm excited to go to work. The official shop hours are 9am, but I usually take my first client at 7:30am every day. Then I'm typically booked solid all day until 6:30pm, except for half an hour for lunch. By the time we clean and cash out it's usually about 7pm when we leave the shop and enjoy our half-hour walk home every night. That's my average day, and I'm thankful for it. I feel lucky to come to a place every day that I love: giving haircuts and shaves, seeing people happy and relaxed when they sit in my chair, having different conversations every half hour, and building a unique and personal relationship with every client. I also feel extremely fortunate to be able to work every day beside Shelley, my wife and business partner, and Noriko – one of the best barbers I've ever had the privilege of working with.

I don't see myself as a big deal in the industry at all. This is a job for me, a beautiful craft of course, but a way to make a living. That's all that matters. If other people respect my work I appreciate it and feel humbled, but I go home with a bag of groceries and that's the end of the day for me! I never take a single day for granted. Everything has a beauty for me, as we say in Persian: each flower has a different scent. When people tell me that I'm recognised worldwide because of my shaving ability, it makes me laugh because I've never seen myself like that. If someone has been doing something for 30 years and isn't good at it then that would be a surprise haha!"

The 'Barber Boom'

"Some time in the last 4 to 5 years I remember a journalist said to me "barbering is coming back, what's your opinion?" My answer was simple: it never went away. Being a barber was my job. There was nothing cool about it. There were no hair shows or awards, we just went to work and made our living. Funny thing is it used to be that some people in the hair industry looked down on barbers. People would even be insulted by the title. Here we are today and everyone wants to call themselves a barber – whether they actually are or not!

In Vancouver there are a few old-timers still going strong. It's great to see them at their age still going at it – soon I'll be one of them! At the same time I like seeing so many young barbers bringing new energy into the profession and helping to make it more popular than ever. When I opened my shop in downtown Vancouver over 11 years ago it was the first and only new barber shop in the downtown area for several years. Now, particularly over the last 5 years or so, I think there are more than 20 new shops opened up.

What will the next 5 years bring? Well, that depends on what you want me to say. The barbering I know has stayed the same and will remain unchanged. If it's the trend you want me to talk about, it'll be around maybe for another 10 to 15 years – and that's great for all of us."

Healthy Competition

"When it comes to titles, I've never won an award as I've never competed against anyone. In my days barbers didn't have titles. We were and still are just barbers. If you check any of my profiles online I've never called myself a master. The best title I could give myself and be happy about it would be the 'neighbourhood barber'. The best award for me is to have my clients come back. For me it's never been about other barbers, it's always about the guy in my chair. Don't get me wrong, in the last few years I've been enjoying the recognition I get, but I'll never see myself differently.

When a new barber shop opens in the neighbourhood, I always stop by to wish them the best and welcome them to the area. As for the 'best barber' I've never believed anyone is the 'best' and I don't think it exists. If the man in your chair likes your work you're good, if he doesn't like it you're not. It's as simple as that. I've always compared it to colours.....you can't choose the best colour, period. One person likes red and someone else likes blue – you can't say blue is better than red, or vice versa, can you?"

Products, Tools, Events, & Publications

"I am not and have never been a product guy. That part of barbering comes from the stylist side of the industry. Having said that, there are definitely some really good products and tools out there. We don't have laws in Canada that force us to shave with gloves and I personally don't think I'd ever feel good about using them, but I don't have anything against people who do. Barbers have been shaving people for millennia without gloves, and in my 30 years I haven't seen anyone have any issues by not wearing them."

The Power of Social Media

"Social media is very important to our industry. I use it regularly, especially Instagram and Facebook. Shelley, my lovely wife, is really good at it and I've learned a lot from her. We've never aimed to be famous, show off, or try to make a 'brand' from our social media account. What we do enjoy is sharing photos and videos of our work so people can see what we do. I want thousands of people who are trying to earn a living by learning how to barber to be able to see what we do for free. Hopefully people who follow us see what we're about, and what we post and share represents exactly who we are."

Any Advice?

"It's not about other barbers it's about your clients. If you pursue this career because you love it, are willing to work hard, take pride in all the details and duties, and treat your employer(s), co-workers, and clients with respect every day, you'll have as much success and satisfaction as you could ever want. That's what barbering means to me."

@farzadthehappybarber

Something that really comes through in this interview is Farzad's humility. He appreciates everything about his job, building up his reputation steadily for years. He has learnt to do one of the things that everyone should do, barber or not and that is to desire the things we already have! With such a long career behind him, it's great to see him getting the recognition and respect he deserves. It couldn't happen to a nicer guy, and it goes to show that being personable and treating people well can help you get ahead in life. He has evolved with the times and with 31 years' experience under his belt, has to be one the most practiced barbers in this book. For him, barbering is not a fashionable career choice, it's been his life for decades.

The longevity of the 'barber boom' is something not all out interviewees can agree on. For Farzad it's immaterial as he will continue in the same vein he always has. I greatly respect his desire to provide free tips through the shop's social media – like a few others have mentioned it's important for the barbers of today to help their future counterparts and one of the best things we can do is share our secrets.

Their shop has a strong social media game however Farzad is aware that his bread and butter are his clients. That's something all prospective barbers need to focus on – followers are great but you need to prioritise the people who pay your bills. The customer's experience evidently means everything to the Happy Barber; trends and fashions come and go but a loyal client base doesn't. The client should be the ultimate judge of our work. It's also great to see a husband and wife team working together. Shelley is more than adept at the business and marketing side of things, and they clearly work well together as evidenced by his busy shop and global reputation.

Overall Farzad's interview provides further evidence that the 'barber boom' is not a Eurocentric phenomenon. Just like their American neighbours, Canada's barbering industry has been growing at a promising rate. If anyone knows, it's the Happy Barber.

T C

Interviews

Chapter 14

Mark Peyton

Owner, Sailor Bup's

My next interview is with another leader in the Canadian market, Mark Peyton. Mark is actually why I travelled to this beautiful country in the first place; we became acquainted on social media and he showed great interest in The Lion's Barber Collective. Since then Mark has been working a great deal to make a Canadian chapter of the Lion's a reality. I spent 3 excellent days in Halifax teaching the amazing Sailor Bup's crew how to make the most of their scissors, and managed to pick Mark's brain on his past, his take on the trade, and a whole lot more.

Backstory

"I've been kicking around for about 5 years, 6 if you count my time as an enthusiast. I'm not taking into account the years of buzz cuts and mohawks I did during my skateboarding days as a teenager though.

I started off by getting into the culture behind the barbershop. It was an old guy I was going to for my hair that started it. I liked the environment, his stories, how he didn't rush a haircut and get you in and out in 15 minutes. I'd had enough of those experiences. As a musician coming off years of playing in bands, touring and working in the music business, I was submerged in the rock n'roll and punk /hardcore scene. I guess I took a step back and realised barbering was one of the oldest trades in history (next to prostitution). Everyone needs a haircut and it was something I could call a career – also I'd have made a horrible prostitute.

I asked a few shops to take me on and they weren't interested because they were worried I'd take their customers from them. So I had to make a go of it myself. I opened my first shop in Halifax over the top of a martini bar, no signage, no nothing. I wanted it to be organic. Maybe it was a matter of taking pride in saying 'I built it' if it was successful. I wanted people to talk about their haircuts and tell people where to get it done. No buyouts of an existing shop, no heavy advertising or marketing. Just down and dirty blue-collar hard work – the way it would've been done in the past. That approach worked.

I had to expand 6 months later and go into a bigger location, hiring more people and focusing on doing things differently due to the change of location. After that shop was established and busy, I was approached by people in a community on the other side of the bridge in a place called Dartmouth. They asked for their own Sailor Bup's because they loved the shop and the environment. They wanted one in their own area. It made perfect sense, so I built a shop completely different from the one in Halifax and started to establish it. Once that was open and sailing independently I had time to sit and read reviews, talk with some customers, and get a few opinions on what I could fix.

The Halifax and Dartmouth shops ran on appointments, and some people were not too happy the walk-in option was no longer there. I was then asked to take over a small location across from the military base. After lots of sleepless nights and way too much overthinking, I decided to pull the trigger and open a small 2 chair walk-in shop. No phone, no credit or debit card, no dedicated social media pages. Just come in, wait for your turn, get your haircut, and go on with your day. I had no real plans of ever seeing things get to where they are now. I wanted one shop, never anything more than that, but I'm humbled, proud, and excited about where we are and how far we've come.

Education was a part of the industry I never thought I'd be involved in. It began when a sales rep who worked for a big local supplier for salons and barbershops emailed me. She asked to schedule a meeting as someone has asked about me. I said sure, and ended up meeting with a guy from Wahl Canada. He said he'd been watching the shop and my work for a while and had an open spot for a Canadian educator. He wanted to offer me the role. As someone who's never happy with a haircut they've done, I was pretty reluctant. I was thinking "how can I educate people when I'm educating myself every day?" He invited me to go to a small show and during the hour long presentation, the guy on stage told a room full of people you only need one clipper and 3 guards to do a guys' haircut. I just about fell off my chair. So we talked and I decided to take the job.

Fast forward a year and I'm at a hair show with Wahl, set up beside a Johnny B and a Reuzel booth. As I was doing a few haircuts and talking to people, I got talking to the Reuzel distributor for Canada. He said Wahl and Reuzel work very closely together because of the ties to Schorem in Rotterdam. He asked me to be on his team. I'd done some training with Schorem and really liked their products, so I said sure. I'm extremely grateful for both of these opportunities. I guess I see it as a testament to the old theory: put your head down, work hard, and good things will come.

Barbering is such a huge part of my life. Cutting my customers hair, getting hyped off my friends in the trade, being challenged to always be better day after day... I'm passionate about what I do and love to share with others. Barbering comes down to being able to connect with the person in your chair, to give them a haircut they like or a shave that looks good. In the future, that's still where I'll be. I continue to make a point of texting my friends from around the world to get them to critique my haircuts and get pointers, or even just say hey.

Education is a huge deal for me, I can't stress it's importance enough. I'm always trying to fill my brain. A lot of my friends poke fun at me, but the truth is I always want to be better. I don't see anything wrong with that. My theory is if you take one thing from a class or lesson, you're further ahead than you were. I don't want my haircuts to look like everyone else's, and I want them to stand out. I combined what I learned from Schorem and Savills and put it to work for a couple years to make sure I was comfortable. I spent some time in California with Shon Lawhon a few months ago to get some pointers from him too, which was great. I've learned so much from others just by watching and asking questions.

There's still so much I want to learn, there's just not enough time. I always try to impress on people that this industry is what you make of it. This is how we make our money, feed our families, pay our bills, and gives us the life we want. If you don't care enough to be better on your next haircut or upgrade your skills, it's just a job, not a career."

The 'Barber Boom'

"The 'barber boom' started a few years ago for sure. When I opened up I wasn't sure if Halifax was going to take to a barbershop that used old chairs. Some were broken, some were torn, some had rust on the bases. They needed regular maintenance but were signs of a time when the trade was done right. Sure I could've restored them, but I wanted to preserve them in their original state for as long as I could. We swear in our shop. We make jokes. If something doesn't make sense or someone doesn't accept our guidelines, we call them on it. That's just barbering. I find a lot of shops are taking to this culture now. A lot of my friends in the industry see the popularisation of male grooming as a fad. But let's be honest, it's good to see guys caring about how they look and if it can create a living for people, do it.

I think barbering will still be around in 5 years' time, but I'm not sure in the same capacity as it is now. I get about 10 messages a week from people who want to be a barber, but I don't think they consider the reality. 6 day work weeks, opening early, staying late, standing on your feet for 10 hours a day without regular breaks, low water consumption, and the health problems that come around with it… it's not for everyone. Especially if they're coming from a very differently structured background. I'm in stage 2 of degenerative disc disease; this is solely due to what I do day in day out. I go home in a lot of pain but I'm taking the proper precautions to ensure I don't land in a wheelchair.

Barbering is an awesome career, it's recession proof. Everyone needs a haircut. That being said when people get into it and realise they don't make a salary and only get paid for the work they do, it's not as attractive. I think we'll see the industry dwindle off a little bit as a result of this. I don't believe any barber should be paid an hourly rate. I think they should be encouraged, supported, and educated to make sure that they're making good money. Those are the people who'll still be here in 5 years."

Healthy Competition

"I don't really take part in the competition thing. I'm in competition with myself, no one else. I get it that most of the time they're friendly and all geared towards having fun, but I've watched people walk away completely defeated. Some people have told me they realised they weren't that good when compared to others, and are now considering a new career. That really sucks to hear. I've seen good barbers give a banging haircut and sh*t customer service, and new barbers give a haircut that needed some work but provide incredible service. In that sense, competitions don't matter to me. All that matters is how the person feels when they leave your chair.

I do have several awards that I've received over my career, and on paper they look good. I'm extremely humbled, grateful, and happy with what I've accomplished so far. That being said at the end of the day all that really matters is my customers leaving happy, telling their friends where they got their haircut, and my crew making a good living.

The 'best' barber is a term I'd personally like to change. I would say 'the inspirational barber' is better. If that was the title, Frank Rimer at Thy Barber in London, Rob and Leen at Schorem in Rotterdam, Joth at Savills in Sheffield, Shon Lawhon at USS Bolsa Chica in California, Farzad at Farzads Barbershop in Vancouver, Jon Roth at Crowsnest Barbershop in Toronto and Michael Martin in Nashville. They're all 'the best' in my eyes.

Barbering is kind of weird in my city. I've travelled the world doing this and it's very different in other countries. I sat in a bar in the UK with people from 2 different shops that were down the street from each other. They were talking about their day, the trade, and just enjoying each other's company. My city is small, less than 500,000 people, so it's pretty cut throat and silly at times. If someone has opportunities another person doesn't or is busier, the sh*t talking gets started. Friendships get formed through negativity. It's all really lame.

We have a barbers association in my province that doesn't even follow their own legislation. They make their own rules and will license/support people that don't pose a threat to them. They are shop owners themselves and hold a vested financial interest in overseeing trade. They've even actively tried to stop education from happening.

I'd really like to see the barbering community (and hair community in general) become more tight knit and supportive here. You can't cut everyone's hair – that's a fact, but I'm pretty sure there are people here who think it's possible. If we're busy, we have no problem sending someone to the shop around the corner. If a customer wants to wait, they'll wait for you. You shouldn't have to slag someone else's work off to keep a customer in your chair. It happens far too often in my area of the world."

Product, Tools, Publications, & Events

"It's the nature of the beast that we need products and tools to change with the times. That being said I'm definitely into classic, traditional barbering. It has stood the test of time. I knew how to do a full haircut using clippers and a comb before I relied on guards. I look for a haircut that will grow out awesome and still be maintainable until I see my customer again 3 weeks later.

I'm a strong believer that the tools and products you use are contributors to your style and should be chosen carefully. I use Wahl because they're solid tools. Sure I work for them, but I was relying on my Senior before I ever signed paperwork with the company. My usual regime is the Ultimate Pro for a detachable blade clipper, the 5 star Senior, the Icon, the cordless Magic Clip and the cordless Super Taper. For trimmers I use the cordless Chromini T-Cuts and the Detailer.

Hair products I'm a little more flexible on. I use Reuzel of course; the line has something for everyone. It's more or less a one stop shop for products. The fact it's formulated and tested by barbers says a lot. I also swear by Steadfast Pomade (which is a hidden gem in the pomade world), the Copacetic Gentlemen's Grooming line released by my friend Joth who owns Savills Barbershop, and the Grant's product line. The Reuzel Grooming Tonic is a must have. I use it for a lot of reasons – not just control, direction and height, but also as a way to double check my work and see if there are any lines, ledges or areas that need to be touched up. The Layrite Grooming

Spray is awesome too, and is a solid prep for pomade. There are so many different products and for anyone to settle on just using one line for all their customers is crazy. Customers want to try new stuff and we are the people they see for that advice."

The Power of Social Media

"I think if any barber doesn't use social media nowadays, they're kind of messing up. I get it that some people don't feel the need to post all their haircuts. I don't. Hell, we can only look at so many bald, faded, side parts. But it is a great way to connect with people in the trade. I value my friendships and relationships, so being able to see something other than their haircuts is pretty rad – especially when I can't talk to them every day. It's kind of like a 'life in pictures' deal.

I use Instagram and Facebook. I find Twitter doesn't work for us at all. The other 2 are much better for interaction and interest. Of course there are negatives to them, but that's just the way life is."

Any Advice?

"This is a loaded gun. This answer may come off as harsh but I'm going to give it anyways. Drop any ego, close the mouth in terms of sh*t talking, never act entitled and think you are owed anything. Ask the questions to people who can answer them, and always strive to be better.

Just remember no matter how good you think you are there's always someone better. Now the brutal truth out of the way, I want people to know this career is incredibly rewarding and fulfilling. You make people look good. If they look good, they feel good. If they feel good, their confidence goes up. If their confidence goes up, their self-esteem goes up. If their self-esteem goes up, their self-worth goes up. There's a lot riding on a haircut. Nail it once and that person will come back to you and refer their friends. At that point, you're building a career."

@markisntabarber
@sailorbupsbarbershop

Mark is one of the most genuine and honest guys I've met in the industry. I greatly appreciated how truthful and expansive he was with all of his answers – he certainly knows what he's talking about. He's made a huge impact around the world, but remains unpretentious and driven to do even more. I especially admired his intention to make the lives of those around him better – not only his customers, but his staff too. This made him a perfect addition to The Lions Barber Collective team. It's also why I was saddened to hear of the negativity surrounding the barbering culture in his hometown. We're lucky to have strong camaraderie in the UK, but understandably competition can cause bad feelings. It's just like Mark said though, one shop can't cut everyone's hair! Thankfully not everyone in the industry feels this way, and I certainly wouldn't be writing this book if that was the case.

He brought up a very valid point which had not been discussed before – the negative aspects of the profession (including the health problems and being self-employed). Many new barbers don't consider these factors. That's why it's vital you have the passion and determination to constantly do better. If not, the over saturation or decline in the market will spell trouble for your career.

Just like Mark, I get messages on a regular basis asking me for advice on how to get into barbering. I usually suggest locations where they can become qualified, as well as advising them to volunteer (as I've mentioned before). I hope they internalise this guidance, but I myself have only ever had one person willing to volunteer their time. Although education is integral, it's fundamental it's paired with experience. You can watch videos, read books, and study techniques, but until you get your hands dirty and see how styles look on different shaped heads and hair types, you can't really understand it. Shadowing another barber is a great way to get ahead and learn things they don't teach you on any course. You have to be proactive in barbering, and the more skilled people you can learn from the better.

Education means a great deal to Mark, and it's certainly going to be a growing market within the next few years. It's admirable that he is so focused on continuing to learn – it's something every creative professional should strive for.

T C
Interviews

Chapter 15

Ollie Nobbs

Founder, Headcase Barbers

After such an excellent trip with some talented barbers overseas, I journeyed back home to meet with the founder of one of the biggest independent barbershop chains across the UK. Ollie Nobbs has had unparalleled success with Headcase Barbers, steadily opening new locations on a national and international scale for years now. When it comes to the business of barbering, there's no question that Ollie has it down.

Backstory

"I've been in the barbering industry for 19 years now, and it's changed beyond all recognition in that time. When I was about 6 I went to a barbershop for the first time. I got my hair cut by a guy called John Gill. He became one of my heroes and was like an older brother to me whilst growing up. My experience with him made me want to be a barber. That being said, it was never a career choice I took too seriously. I completed my education and pursued other paths before returning back.

When I started my journey there weren't any barber courses to attend. I went to college to study A levels, and began to lead myself down the same path my father had walked. I hated it. I met a girl who was a hairdresser which led me back to the trade. I quit my A levels, enrolled in a Technical College and got an apprenticeship. I really struggled. Don't get me wrong – I enjoyed the people I worked with, I just hated doing ladies hair. I nearly quit a few times but my mum and dad talked me into seeing it through.

When I finished my apprenticeship I went on holiday with my grandparents to think about my future. I was actually considering becoming a PE teacher as I loved sport. Whilst I was on holiday John Gill, the man I had looked up to since a young age, fell off his motorbike and broke his arm. He needed a barber, I could cut (just about) so I decided to help him out. His call changed my life and came in the one week window I'd given myself to decide my future. I came back from holiday, quit my apprenticeship and went to work for him. He stood there pointing out where I needed to improve and showed me how to hold clippers properly. He basically taught me how to be a barber. This was 1999 – no one got opportunities like that. It's comparable to trying to become a tattooist today, you have to know someone who's willing to teach you.

I had a 6 month deal. He would heal in this time and a lady was returning after maternity leave which meant there was no place left for me. This meant I had 6 months to train and find my own shop. I ended up finding a little place in Godalming, Surrey. My dad secured a loan for me and I opened Headcase. My brother Martin started a few weeks later and I trained him while we were quiet – although it didn't stay that way for long. We built the business to focus on great customer service and clientele interaction. People loved that we were brothers, as well as the music we played and the general atmosphere. Next I bought in my best mate Marc and another barber Mandy joined, so I looked for a second shop. I opened in Haslemere, Surrey in 2003 and launched the website – nowadays I can't imagine opening a shop without one! No Instagram, no Facebook, no YouTube, no social media…It's hard to imagine.

Around 2004 I became the Hair Doctor for the Good Barbers Guide, and then in 2006 I joined the WAHL artistic team, taking over their wet shaving courses after Simon Shaw was promoted to global art director. Throughout this time I continued to build on the shops' success, and in 2008 I opened my third place in Farnham, Surrey. All the locations were really busy and we had a great team of 12 barbers.

I always wanted to make the barbering industry better than it was. I wanted people to actually decide to be barbers. It bloody annoyed me that people ended up doing this amazing job because they couldn't be hairdressers. It was such an insult. So in 2012 I decided to look at franchising. I joined with 2 other guys who understood my vision and we all bonded really well. Since 2012 we've gone from 3 shops to 22, spanning 3 countries (England, South Africa, and Netherlands). We have a master franchise finding stores in Ireland which will be the 4th country, and have the next 18 shops lined up. We're also about to sign our 5th country, welcoming Sweden into the family. Our main focus is to develop the industry and make barbershops accessible to the right people, who otherwise might not be able to open their own place. Later this year we'll be looking to launch our Headcase Academy, which will be groundbreaking.

From the minute I decided to call my company 'Headcase', I knew it had to be followed by 'International'. In 2000 having an international business seemed impossible, but I wanted to leave myself room to grow. If I called it that, then one day I'd have to make it international somehow. I knew that if I could get one shop then I could get 2, and if I could get 2 then I could get 3 and so on. I knew from college I wanted to be a barber, and I hated the way barbershops looked at the time. I wanted a place that I'd love to go to. Every shop we open, I try and introduce a new idea. I try to continue pushing new concepts, keeping Headcase ahead of the game. I'm terrified of standing still and research and development is always at the forefront of my mind. I compare Headcase to the way an F1 team runs and am always on the lookout for milliseconds in improvements. We have our own custom built epos system that my brother and I developed. This is constantly being updated to find the best use of information and keep our shops as profitable as possible.

Headcase is a co-operative franchise; this term best describes the way we operate. We are not a cookie cutter model like people believe franchises to be. Each Headcase is individual and reflects the owners and barbers within the shops. It's what gives it its own culture and keeps the experience authentic. I decided to franchise because I could see more of an impactful growth down this route. I can reach more people who need help, and can connect with driven individuals who want to be part of something amazing. We have an incredible network (currently around 80+ barbers) and we all help out with different day-to-day issues. It's an incredible way to develop. Being part of such a large group comes with so many benefits, and I'm constantly finding ways to save my partners money. We have some excellent deals with some of the largest players in the game and the opportunities are endless.

I branched into South Africa because the Master Franchisee there (Scott) used to work for me in Godalming. He purchased the Godalming shop from me in 2012, and then moved back to his native home and wanted to take Headcase back with him. I purchased the

Godalming location back from him, and he used the money to open Headcase in Johannesburg in 2015. Nothing like Headcase exists over there and it's taken off like wild fire. The shops in the Netherlands came about because a guy from there, Wouter, found us and loved what he saw. He was looking for a fresh challenge and got in touch. In 2 years he's opened 2 shops and is looking to open more. The barbering scene in the Netherlands is very similar to the UK, so the synergy and business models work very well.

I think of ways to evolve strategy daily. Psychology is at the front of my thoughts so I try and understand people in every location we open. I want to inspire my team to push, to try and help people better their lives. I want to have a company that people love and want to be part of"

The 'Barber Boom'

"Barbering really took off around 5 years ago, and the acceleration has been unreal. Social Media has been absolutely key to this growth. The barbering community is now in touch and competitive, which drives the standard and culture. Finally people want to be barbers.

What is the future of barbering? That's a hard question to answer. There's a bit of a power struggle at the moment with the market leaders. This might result in transforming barbering into more of a hairdressing-type field, becoming more polished. If the large product corporations (L'Oréal etc.) decide to really get involved, that's where it'll head as the money and marketing will drive it in that direction. If they instead decide to dabble and not commit, I think it'll keep its feel and culture. We'll see training academies improve and more popular men's product lines strengthen their positions. This will improve the standard throughout the entire spectrum. Trainees will be shop-ready from the academies (something that doesn't happen at the moment). At Headcase we see so many barbers leave courses and come to us thinking they're shop-ready because that's what they've been told and sold. This leads to feelings of disappointment which is a shame. The industry needs regulation in some form and I'm sure this will happen. I'm excited to see what the future holds."

Healthy Competition

"Titles or awards are things I've never chased after. My primary focus has been the relentless development of my business and how I can improve it for my customers. I always focused on working inside my walls. You need to remember that prior to around 5 years ago the barbering industry was a shadow of its present form. There was no Instagram, no real barbering publications that pushed the industry, not many competitions to showcase work... I didn't see them as necessary for the growth of Headcase. In the last 5 years I've been so busy developing my company and franchise that I don't have time to get involved. The guys within Headcase are free to compete and we actively support their adventures. More and more barbers that join us are from hairdressing backgrounds really enjoy them, so I encourage it. We're currently putting together a dedicated competition team made up of members from all over the Headcase family.

I've looked at big names in the barbering world today and I find it difficult to place myself. I don't do Magazine shoots. I don't get involved with workshops. I'm not linked to any Expos. This is on purpose. My focus has been on business development for my brand. I'm not an educator, I don't want to be one. I don't want to seek the status of 'celebrity barber', whatever that is. I think I'm one of the business leaders in the industry. No-one in the U.K. has opened as many barbershops as I have. I've designed every one of the 18 shops here and personally shop-fitted almost all of them. I've helped find staff and developed every single location. By the end of this year I'll have been responsible for another 18 shop openings, finding another 18 ways to push barbering further."

Products ,Tools, Publications, & Events

"Products have a very important role in Headcase. They represent the shops, the barbers, and the clients. They need to be culturally right for the location. This is why we have multiple product lines throughout the 18 shops. We aren't glued to one company. We've dabbled in the past with some of the giant industry leaders and it simply hasn't worked, so we moved back to the products that our barbers were talking about. At the end of the day, the products have to be right for the clients.

Tools are great now; the American influence is game changing. The UK has to catch up or the manufacturers need to hurry up and launch them here. God knows why they don't. I really like the new cordless stuff, I've always hated draping cables over clients. Foil shavers are a good tool – although not new tech, the design is great.

Shows, competitions, and expos are great for inspiring for barbers. A few years ago all barbers had was Salon International, which was more focused on females. The new barbering expos are great. They're still quite new, and young barbers in particular get a lot from them. As far as choosing who 'the best' is, I don't think it matters. The top guys all do amazing work. As long as people keep getting inspired, that's what's important. Nowadays inspiration is at our fingertips.

When it comes to events, Headcase has been to several over the last few years. They're great fun and it's a good opportunity to meet barbers and network. I really like the structure and scale of Barber Connect. I'm going to America this year to attend a few expos there to see how those guys do it, from what I see they look amazing. We plan on opening Headcase in the USA in the next few years, so these different events are important to experience. The GBBB has an exciting feel and it'll be fun to see how big it will get."

The Power of Social Media

"Social media is a great tool for us. Different platforms work for different needs. The business Facebook pages are generally customer facing, Instagram is more advertising our work to the world and showing our Headcase shops. The other media platforms don't have a lot of impact for us really, and are more for fun."

Any Advice?

"The advice I'd give to new and aspiring barbers is to absorb as much information as possible. The possibility to learn these days is everywhere. Open your phone and you can see amazing things. There are no excuses. Watch a lot of YouTube – the videos and tutorials are awesome. Absorb the information, practice on friends, and try and replicate what you see on your courses. Don't rush your training. You need to train your eyes to see lines and shape. Get practical cutting in as often as possible so you're comfortable with your tools. Then your hands and eyes can work together, and you'll improve quickly.

Customers don't want fast work, they want great work. You'll never get great by cutting corners. Focus on seeing the errors in your cuts, be honest with your work and correct your mistakes. I always think that if my work was going to be photographed, would I be happy with it? Stay relentless in the quality of work you do. Above all, love what you do and everything will be great. This is an amazing industry, and it's never been better than right now."

@ollie_nobbs

Speaking with Ollie was a refreshing experience. He's not looking to be a famous barber, educator, or platform artist. He's focused entirely on his business, and this has led him to have great success. Fame doesn't necessarily equate to fortune, and Ollie has a seemingly limitless commitment to improving Headcase as a whole. That's not to say he doesn't see the benefits of social media, competitions, etc. but it's clear his attention is squarely aimed at constantly evolving and growing his dream. This constant quest for marginal gains is admirable – it's the small changes that contribute to the larger success over time.

Ollie made some interesting observations in terms of the industry giants and how their actions can basically dictate the future of barbering. Ideally I think a lot of barbers would prefer independent products, academies, tools and shops to build on the culture we've spent years creating. It's with the support of companies like Headcase that we can ensure independent entities continue to grow – just like Ollie I use a mix of brands and don't tie myself down to one, and your choices should be based on what works for your customers and for you.

I learnt a lot about the man behind the brand throughout this interview. Ollie comes at the industry from a different perspective, and the story of Headcase is an inspirational one. It goes to show that there are multiple paths to success in this profession.

TC

Interviews

Chapter 16

Carl Blake

Wahl Academy Team Member

Still in the UK, I wanted to find out a little more about the world of competition, and who better than a former judge of Wahl Barber of the Year, Carl Blake? He's a Wahl guru and educator with a long history in barbering. He has had a respectable career spanning decades, so I was excited to pick his brain about all things barbering.

Backstory

"I've been in the industry for 30 years and own Blake's Grooming in West Chiltington, Sussex. I started in the 1980's after enrolling in the YTS training scheme. As soon as I qualified I was eager to work with men's hair so I switched to barbering, working in a succession of barbershops in East Sussex before opening my first shop in Lewes. After 3/4 years I wanted more from the industry, so I sold Blades and relocated to London. Whilst there I was lucky enough to work in some fantastic barber shops, as well as meeting some amazing people along the way. One of these people was Wahl artistic director, Simon Shaw. I met him at the prestigious British Hairdressing Awards dinner in 2006, having been nominated for Men's Hairdresser of the Year myself.

After chatting with Simon he gave me his card and said to give him a call. The outcome was becoming a new member of the Wahl artistic team. It was a huge step in my career and one I grabbed with both hands. After much nurturing and ongoing training, I've now been a member of the team for 10 years. This role takes me all over the globe to attend various exhibitions and seminars teaching new clipper techniques. Juggling this with running my own business makes for a very busy lifestyle.

In my own salon I don't tend to see myself any differently to my staff. I like my customers to see us all on a level playing field. When I'm out of the salon I feel very privileged to be part of the Wahl artistic team. We've all worked very hard to build the team into one of the most prestigious and professional barbering groups in the world. As far as where I see myself in the industry, for me it's more about us as a team than me individually"

The 'Barber Boom'

"The rise in barbering started to happen around 10 years ago. In my opinion this was spurred on by a change in the workplace 20 years before... equality. It seemed to take a few years for men to wake up to the fact that women took more care in their appearance in a professional setting. As men became exposed to more women working, they started to want to take more care in their appearance to mirror their female counterparts. Men's grey, dreary suits were gone...as were the same, boring, basic haircuts the majority of men were sporting at the time. This gave way to the modern day man; a man with more flair and style incorporated into his everyday life, and a sharp haircut is firmly on his list of essentials.

With the rise in barbering showing no signs of slowing down, I do see somewhat of a divide happening in the next 5 years. We're now seeing many more men's hairdressers opening – by this I mean a place a guy can go to be totally groomed. Men can have a haircut/shave/beard shape/skin treatments/wax/manicure etc. as well as grooming advice and multiple products. At the other end of the spectrum is your standard barbershop which can be found on almost any high street. The code of practice here is a client takes a seat for a while and has a haircut by the first available barber. There is next to no advice or up selling services and no aftercare. These 2 cultures have created a divide in the industry that in my opinion has already begun."

Healthy Competition

"When it comes to competitions there are so many out there now in barbering, which can only be a good thing. I try to get my staff to enter as many as possible. This can only inspire them to do a better job on a day-to-day basis.

Although I don't think it really matters who's the best, the rules generally state if you win a particular competition you're the best of those who entered. I think it's more important to those people individually than trying to put someone at the top of the tree, so to speak."

Products, Tools, Publications, & Events

"Working with Wahl (the leading clipper brand in the world) I'm lucky enough to see and use many new tools that come onto the market before they hit the high street. I have one word to describe recent tool development...wow! The new wave of tools are making such an incredible impact on the industry; cordless items being the biggest influence in recent years.

As for products, well where do I start? There are so many different brands nowadays I tend to listen to my clients and try to cater to their needs, after all it's them we need to keep happy. My favourite product would have to be the Wahl Clay – number 19 it's so malleable and can be used on almost any hair type. My favourite tool is the Wahl Cordless Magic Clip as it's perfect for fades/blending/tapering.

My favourite magazine has to be *Modern Barber*, Rachel Gould does a fantastic job with it. The best event by far is Salon International – not only because it's 3 days presenting on our biggest stage of the year, but also because we get to run the live final of our competition, Wahl Barber of the Year!"

Any Advice?

"My advice for any aspiring barbers would be to try to improve one thing every day/week/month. Don't try to run before you can walk, master the basics, and the rest will follow."

@blakie007

Carl's career has been carved in part by a chance meeting at an event; this details the importance of always acting professionally and in a pleasant manner in any and all situations. We all know that first impressions mean a lot, and you can never make a second one. We must never underestimate our actions in a specific moment, as they can create opportunities in the future. Carl's wholly positive opinion of competitions differs in part with some of the previous interviewees. I guess for him competitions have opened a lot of doors, even if he didn't win on the day so it makes sense for him to encourage his staff to do the same.

I was also most intrigued by Carl's assessment of the 'barber boom' being popularised as a result of growing sexual equality in the workplace. The term 'metrosexual' was coined many years ago, and it could be argued it was a major catalyst in the 'barber boom'. His description of a split in the culture of barbering is another novel point. Shops that are focused on male grooming are relatively new, so it'll be interesting to see how they progress in the coming years.

As a barber with 30 years of experience his insight into the changing workplace, equality, men's approach to grooming, and the trade as a whole is invaluable. We can learn so much from looking to our past, and people like Carl are evidence of that.

TC

Interviews

Chapter 17

Alan Beak

Ruger Barber, International Educator

When it comes to being detail orientated, there's one barber in the UK that commits to perfection every time. He has driven the industry forward becoming an inspiration to many; he has even worked with high profile footballers like Sergio Agüero. It is of course, Alan Beak. He and his brother, Reece are major influencers of the 'barber boom' and his Ruger barbershops have gone from strength to strength. Not only is he one of the best presenters and educators in the business, he's also kind, effortlessly cool, sincere, and supportive –often volunteering his time to help me and many others (time is, as we all know, a priceless commodity). There was no question that I had to interview him for this project.

Backstory

"I started working in a barbers when I was 12 years old. I'd sweep up, make coffees, and do all the general things a junior does to ensure the shop runs smoothly. I used to even wash the owners cars if the shop was quiet. I like to keep myself busy. In between working at the salon I started bar work and progressed to being the overall manager of a restaurant. Having a love of food, I then trained to be a chef. Once I got to a certain point I decided to get back into barbering and went hell for leather. I made it my hobby, put my heart and soul into it, and worked every day to get where I am today. 2 years ago I was given a 'British Master Barber' award, the rest of them I'm still working on. I spent some time teaching at a college, but left because I thought the standard of qualified students was very low. I'd love to see this rise significantly.

Barbering is an art form and a very skilled trade – its time it's treated that way. I'd love to play a part in making this happen. In the future I'd love to have my own brand RUGER (which I started with my younger brother Reece a few years ago) grow as much as possible. He and I work incredibly hard doing what we do. We focus on creating a barbershop vibe that invites all walks of life, offering the best services possible in a cool, relaxed, high-end environment. We're all about standards and pushing the progression of the industry, so advancing our tuition is something I'm looking forward to doing. So many people have inspired me and I'd like to be able to inspire others.

We've been incredibly lucky to visit every corner of the UK and Ireland. We've done New York and Dubai and have plans to go to Spain, Holland and Shanghai. It's amazing where barbering can take you. Still to this day I'm overwhelmed at the opportunities we've created and there's no limit to where we can take it."

The 'Barber Boom'

"I suppose it was about 8 years ago that I started to see boys and men becoming more concerned about their appearance. This was the catalyst for me to start honing my skills and learning as much as possible. I made sure my range of knowledge in all aspects of hair was as wide as it could be, including study into longer cuts and work to create more detailed layering and sectioning. Then came the US influence in the form of fading which combined with classical, European cutting. That was when I knew it was time to start merging different techniques and experimenting. The more we as barbers could offer, the more people wanted.

The standards of haircuts right now are insanely high, all I can see happening in the future is this getting even higher. This can only be a good thing because it means the industry will continue to progress – which has always been my main prerogative since first starting to cut hair. There are barbershops popping up everywhere these days, which is good but it would be nice not to see a case of over saturation. We should be focusing on quality and not quantity. As barbering is now catching up to lady's hairdressing, I think in 5 years' time the split between men's and women's hairdressing at shows and throughout media and magazines will be equal."

Healthy Competition

"Barbering competitions are a great way for people to showcase their work. As long as the judging process is professional and impartial, the outcome can be amazing for those who excel in them. Competitions get a lot of bad press as people think they're biased (past experience has shown me they can be) but in the right hands and done the right way, I'm always up for helping people to get their work out there. Some people just deserve a lucky break. I know exactly how much hard work goes into self-progression and how challenging it is, so if that's what it takes to give people a helping hand then I'm game.

I have plenty of idols. New ones pop up every day – people who I see coming through the ranks, getting the recognition they deserve. I end up watching them at shows. Others aren't big on social media and are very much unsung heroes, but I still love to watch their progression. I admire seeing individuality whether it be through cuts, finishing, or photography. If I had to pick one idol it has always been Kevin Luchmun. He combines every aspect of cutting and styling with high fashion, traditional, and contemporary styles. He isn't one to follow trends, he creates them"

Products, Tools, Publications, & Events

"With time, products and tools have advanced to reflect the demand and changes in style. Equipment has become sharper and more powerful to help us cope with higher volumes of people and to result in faster cutting times. Our job has had to become more time efficient and accurate, so clippers use motors that cut closer to the scalp to ensure the precision of fades. In over 10 years I've used every single product and piece of equipment on the market, and at the moment my entire arsenal consists of Wahl clippers and tools. They meet my everyday needs and more. There are clippers for every aspect of cutting and their tools help me to do my job to the highest standard.

After testing products for around 2 years, I was approached by a well-known white label company. I got along better with these more than any company I'd ever used previously. 6 years on after striking up a brilliant relationship, I was given the opportunity to start formulating products that Reece and I wanted to use on a daily basis to create the look we were striving to achieve. It's taken a very long time to create an exclusive range that's perfect for every client.

There are too many shows to mention that I'm incredibly proud of. Opening the Barber Shop Connect event BarberCon in New York for the second year was an amazing achievement. As is working with the Great British Barber Bash as team captain: travelling the world, headlining each show, conducting workshops to thousands of aspiring barbers and hairdressers… it gives me a huge sense of satisfaction. It's great to know I'm giving something back and hopefully making a difference. Appearing on stage on numerous occasions at Pro Hair Live and Salon International was a great privilege too.

The publication range we have still blows my mind. Seeing our faces and the brand on front covers and page spreads in magazines such as *Modern Barber Mag, The Barber magazine, Barber Evo* and *Barber NV* makes me feel incredibly proud."

The Power of Social Media

"Social media is a great platform for someone to express themselves through pictures and to showcase their work. It shows individuality, as each page is a reflection of the person behind it. I use my social media to show the world new things. I try, more than anything, to use it as a tool to create relationships. These relationships can start off simple (such as a like on a picture), and then move onto a comment praising a good cut. It also lets you see what else is being done all around the world, allowing you to compare your work and make yourself a better barber. I like to see somebody do something new and then try to emulate it myself. Vice versa, I like to do new things and hope to inspire other people. People from all round the world see your work and it can open doors you never thought possible. I've been lucky enough to cut the hair of extremely high profile clients, travel all round the world, and meet my idols all down to social media.

Hard work and consistency in your online presence is so important. We're a nation of phone users and lovers of social media. More people than ever imagined can see your work, so persistence is key when it comes to being noticed. High profile clients are to me just simply a client – somebody who likes your work and wants to put your skills to the test. If they like it they always call back."

Any Advice?

"The best advice I can give anyone would be to focus on what you're doing, don't be deterred by the actions of everyone else. Focus on your own work, and in that respect stay individual. Don't copy other people – just because it worked for them doesn't mean it's going to work for you. Stay genuine and organic, this will always prevail. It will take time so be persistent. Have goals, realistic and achievable ones. Work on each one until you reach them all. Once they're done, set new goals to push yourself even further. Step out of your comfort zone and don't be afraid to take risks."

@alan_beak

Alan's journey in hairdressing has taken him on a different route to many of the other individuals in this book. He turned his hobby into his career, which is a great basis as it shows his passion. My career went from strength when I spent my time out of the shop thinking about the industry and doing research. If you love what you do and it becomes part of your interests outside of work, it can only be a good thing. Like I have mentioned before in this book, we all have 168 hours a week. It's how we use them that determine what we achieve.

RUGER has a prominent presence in both traditional and modern media. Getting yourself noticed on social media is important, and alongside a barber's scissors and clippers should be a high quality DLSR camera with that trusty 50mm lens to help best showcase their cuts. Cutting the hair of high profile clients is something a lot of us dream of, yet achievable to most. It's down to a mixture of timing, relationships, and skill. Being well-known on social media can certainly help with this type of exposure. Alan's observation that American styles have merged with traditional European cuts is most interesting. That's another great thing about social media – the merge of cultures and the resulting trends it creates. Fades have been integral in the popularisation of barbering, perfected for years by afro and urban hairdressers. This has meant the modern barber has to have a whole new skill set to keep up.

A lot of the techniques that Alan demonstrates can be linked to the development of new tools and products. There's a huge choice out there now, and it can become a bit of a minefield. Variation is important so it's always a good idea to try a vast range and find what works for you and your customers. I'm pretty sure most barbers' dream is to have their own bespoke range of products, and Alan and RUGER have done just that. Designing your own products offers a more personal touch for your clients, as you can let them know exactly what goes into the manufacturing of it and how it should be used. Retention is one of the main pillars of a barber's success, and providing your own product is another variable you can control to ensure customer satisfaction.

Alan is one of the catalysts in the popularisation of barbering, and it's great to see he's still very goal orientated. It's important to take time out, sit down, and think about what you want to achieve so you can figure out the necessary steps. Each time you reach a goal, it makes you more motivated to push for the next one. Clearly this is something Alan has done and continues to do. His work is always progressing, even when it seems there's no room left for improvement. He's constantly pushing himself and inspiring others, so it was wonderful to get his take on the topics.

T C

Interviews

Chapter 18

Kieron Price

Raw: Image Barbershop, Andis Educator

The next barber I talked to is possibly the best in the business when it comes to mastering YouTube. He works with one of the biggest companies around and has been all over the world at some of the biggest events on the planet. I've been lucky enough to know Kieron for quite some time. We spend our time discussing our 2 favourite things: hair and wrestling (in fact I'm sure he wouldn't be averse to showing you a picture of him in his wrestling gear). Mastering the field of YouTube is no mean feat, so I wanted to find out how he has achieved something that has eluded so many others – not only getting himself noticed by huge barbering companies, but also getting people to hit the subscribe button.

Backstory

"I started when I was 13 as a Saturday boy in a hairdressers, so I've been in the business for about 16 years all in all. When I began my career it was as a hairdresser. I finished my NVQ Level 3 but it wasn't fulfilling my expectations. I found I had a lot more fun doing men's hair, which prompted me to pursue it. I started as a barber when I was 19 or 20 and haven't looked back. I was lucky enough to have an 8 year stint at Baldy's Barbers, and became a recognisable face in the barbering world via my YouTube hair tutorials. These have led to many other opportunities. I'm now an international educator for Andis and travel the world teaching cutting and shaving. Last year I took a big leap and bought my own shop (Raw Image Barbershop).This has been open for around 10 months and I couldn't be happier. I also won British Master Barber of the year 2015 which was amazing!

My role with Andis is as an international educator. I fell in love with the company when we did a shoot with them, and since then I've become a big part of their family – along with my partner in crime Baldy, who himself is now Lead Educator for the UK. I just love the tools and I'm so fortunate to work with them.

YouTube is funny, I love it but it's so up and down. I mean I make a video and I'm thinking "This is the one!" and then I put it out and it doesn't do as well as the others…it's all down to the viewers. The main thing with YouTube is consistency, a good camera, and a decent microphone. Myself and Arichman Perez both do YouTube videos – he's has only been doing it 2 months and one of his videos has already hit 100,000 views! It's about being different…find a niche in the market and go for it!"

The 'Barber Boom'

"I think the 'barber boom' started about 5 years back… that seems so long ago now. I started my Instagram account as an online look book for my clients and it just blew up, it's awesome that it's come this far. As for where my barbering is going, you know, I actually get asked this a lot and my answer is always the same. As long as my family is happy and healthy and I'm still enjoying it, then I hope to be doing exactly what I'm doing right now. Honestly I'm really happy with everything. I don't ask for a lot – I just love to teach and inspire. Right now I see myself as educator; someone who can inspire the next generation of barbers to give it a go. I love seeing young talented barbers come out of nowhere – it's awesome to experience and hopefully I can be part of that process."

Healthy Competition

"Healthy competition is always good! I like the fact that there are competitions where people can showcase their work and battle other barbers – but I dislike all the hate in the industry, and there's a lot of it. I have a few favourite barbers but it's down to personal preference…they might not be the best in other people's eyes but they inspire me. I'm no way the best barber – I'm not even close! There are a million barbers who're better than me; that gives me fire in my belly to always strive to be better. Always make a positive a negative. People get jealous and it shouldn't be like that, we're all doing the same thing…trying to make our customers happy and put food on our tables."

Products, Tools, Publications, & Events

"My current set up is all Andis (obviously), US Pro cordless, Ionicas and foil shavers. My favourite tool has to be the Slim Line Pro Li's, they're great for a diverse range of styles.

The 'barber boom' has made it so there are so many different opportunities to network and get together. My favourite show by far was LBS New York! I friggin' loved that show! I left my heart there. Everyone showed love to one another – there was no hate, just loads of pictures taken, handshakes, and hugs...It was an event where everyone felt at home and wasn't being judged. Industry events are a must and we're getting more and more every year. It's great but please people, if you're coming to an event leave your ego and attitude at home. Come and enjoy them, have a laugh, and learn – that's what they're here for."

Any Advice?

"To any barber starting out I would say that you must not forget the 3 H's...head, heart and hand. If you can think it in your head and your heart believes you can do it, your hands will do the work for you. This attitude will get you far in life. Remember always be humble and enjoy yourself. It's a fun industry to be in, share your work on social media and always, always be yourself!"

@kieronthebarber

As Kieron says, healthy competition is great, and winning a competition can be a huge stepping stone in someone's career. Some are happy to have achieved it, then sit back and do nothing with the win, whereas others use it to springboard themselves into product endorsement, education, or into the media. Competitions are a huge part of our industry, and winning can tell you a lot about the kind of barber you want to be. I know barbers who have achieved incredible things and travel the world without winning a single competition, but there's no denying it can make certain types of success easier.

Consistency is important in all walks of life – including video blogging. I know from the content I subscribe to, new footage is uploaded daily or weekly. It takes work to find the time to do this, so I try and support as much as I can by sharing and commenting on videos I like. Most barbers use YouTube as an educational tool, but few really make the most of it in terms of marketing. Kieron has made a great impact, but like he said it's down to the viewers. If you want to get the highest views you need good tools, skill, a camera and audio equipment, and personality of course! The higher quality your video, the better viewing it will make. We are aesthetic creatures, especially us barbers. If it looks good chances are we'll watch it.

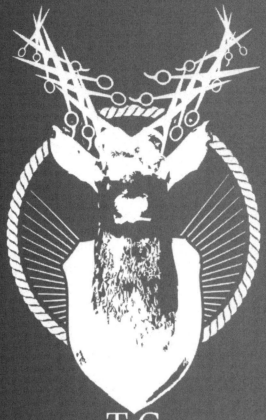

TC

Interviews

Chapter 19

Lawrence Fo

International Educator

For my next interview, I wanted to pick the brain of one of my best friends and someone who has influenced and inspired me to no end. I never fail to learn from Lawrence and he's one of the most skilled men on the planet with a pair of clippers in his hand. And one of the most genuine and kind guys I've ever met. Overtime I've seen his technique progress, picking up every new product or tool on the market and adding it to his arsenal. I've been fortunate enough to have shared a stage, hotel rooms, and many international journeys with him, and it's always been a pleasure.

Lawrence is a truly humble guy and an excellent educator. As soon as he opened a social media account, his following and work offers went through the roof at a global scale. He was aware of The Lions Barber Collective and the work we were trying to do, and has been a great supporter of the cause. Later on he opened up and shared his story with me; it's amazing to hear about his journey and how he has turned his life around, becoming the award-winning international barber and educator he is today:

Backstory

"I've been a barber for over 21 years, so I've seen a lot in my time. I first started cutting my friend's hair when I was at school just using a pair of my dad's clippers, mimicking what I'd seen the barber do on my own hair. Then after a few bent truths and exaggerations I managed to get work at a number of barbershops. This was where I started to properly learn what I was doing by watching and surrounding myself with good barbers who were willing to share their techniques.

Over the next 10 years I worked around the country, plying my trade and making a living. When I was asked to work at Gregory Max Barbers in Milton Keynes by my good friend Greg Mcerlane, I was flattered as I was a massive fan of their work and style. At that point I didn't have social media or anything like that, but within a few months my career had changed. I was invited to Asia to do a guest spot in Macau, and I also joined the Great British Barber Bash working at shows around the UK. I was then asked to join the Lions Barber Collective, which meant so much to me as I've suffered mental health issues since my teens. I was fortunate last year to travel abroad a lot, educating, doing photo shoots, and attending barber-related events. I was also incredibly lucky as I've only entered one competition (The British Barber Association Hall of Fame) and managed to win it in February 2016.

The 'Barber Boom'

"Personally I would say it was about 5 years ago that I became aware of a rise in barbering. It's a really exciting time to be part of this amazing industry and I think it's just getting started. I feel this boom in barbering will continue and bring further recognition to all of us for the skills involved and the hard work we put in."

Healthy Competition

"When it comes to the choosing the 'best barber', I feel that the only people whose opinion matters are the customers."

Products, Tools, Publications, & Events

"Product wise, I've always been minimal. I prefer to use a pre-blow drying aid and either hairspray or powder. As far as tools are concerned, it's all changed. Gone are the days of having just one pair of clippers, one brush and one pair of scissors. Now we all have a bag full of different tools. I use all brands when it comes to clippers, but mostly Andis. My favourite scissors have to be Mattaki."

To create my fades I use an Andis Supra ZR with a "00000" blade, Andis Slim Line Pro, Oster Fast Feeds, Andis foils, and Wahl Cordless Magic Clip. It's not the only way, but it's the method and tools I use every day. It's what I've been doing for my whole career and it works for me. That's what's important. Find out what works for you."

The Power of Social Media

"I don't know what I did before social media. I prefer Instagram, as it gets your work seen by such a large audience and really can open a lot of doors and make barber-related connections possible. I've had so many inspirations in barbering and we would need a whole different chapter for me to list them all, but off the cuff in no particular order would include Tom Chapman, Alan and Reece Beak, Harry and Rhys Green, Alan Findley, Greg Mcerlane, Frank Rimer, Jody Taylor, the whole Irish contingent, and last but by no means least my better half Karla Elton.

I've been so fortunate to travel since starting my social media accounts. Up to now my best trip would be the last tour we did together with El Patron, an American men's product range. It started in Reno, Nevada and finished in San Francisco, California at the Golden Gate Bridge. Great people, great haircuts, great laughs, and great memories."

Any Advice?

"My number one piece of advice would be stay humble and stay true to your own style."

@onelovebarber

One of the main reasons I admire Lawrence is no matter how much success he has, he remains modest. It's great to be grounded, but you should also be aware of your achievements. In the UK we often find it difficult to talk about ourselves and accept praise –in the states they seem to be way more comfortable with this concept. From my experience they openly explain what they do, where they're been, and their achievements, and expect you to do the same – after which they'll support and congratulate you on any success. There's certainly something to take from that attitude.

I've seen Lawrence work many times, and his fade techniques are second to none. It's what he's famous for. His work is phenomenally smooth and aesthetically stunning, so it was great for him to share a shopping list of tools to create the perfect fade. Having the basic skill is important, but there's so much room for

150

creativity, individuality, and choosing your own path when it comes to this craft.

It's a huge honour to make Lawrence's top ten, and the fact he has made so many connections through social media further shows the importance this medium has for us. It has opened doors on a global scale for me as well, allowing me to travel from my seaside home in Devon to countries all around the world. These opportunities are in part due to my online exposure. The trip Lawrence mentioned above is particularly important to me, because that's when I started the journey that is this book.

Lawrence has also been a huge part of the Lions Barber Collective and has openly spoken about his mental health. His sharing of his journey is not only brave, it helps raise awareness and lowers the stigma around mental health – the core aims for the collective. He has come through everything life has thrown at him and is a hugely successful barber who has taught all across the globe, been featured on national television, and has graced the stage at the biggest events. He really is an inspiration.

TC

Interviews

Chapter 20

Sindi Devitte

Owner, Rio Barbers & Barbersclan

My final trip on this journey led me to Brazil. I was here in a teaching capacity, working alongside the famed barber Sindi Devitte. As one of the most famous barbers in Brazil it seemed like a no-brainer that I should get her views down on paper.

Sindi is the owner of Rio Barbers in Coventry, a huge part of Revista QG magazine, and the owner of the incredible Barbersclan academy located here in Brazil. I've been fortunate to have had a friendship with Sindi for a while; she has supported The Lions Barber Collective and has been a huge help for the cause. She's generous, kind, passionate, cares about education, and is doing all she can to reshape the barbering world in her country and beyond.

Backstory

"I've been in the industry for 16 years – only barbering, no hairdressing at all. I'm a barber through and through, from day one on the shop floor up to now.

Before I had my kids I studied journalism at University. This is why I came to England – I wanted a degree in my second language. I had my kids at a young age so I had to give up my career. I wanted to do something that was not so difficult to do whilst having children, so I started barbering in Brazil. There was no basics and no real education for barbering at that time. It was very poor, still is very poor. That's why I started my project here.

I then came to the UK as my partner was English, and started working in Asian barbershops. The white English shops were very hard to get into – even though I'm white I was still seen as foreign. In the Asian shops I learn a lot! I learnt the fades, the lines, and stuff that in some courses is very hard to learn.

Over time my haircuts improved and I got a job in the best barbershop in the city. It was really, really nice to work there. I worked there for 5 years and then decided to buy my own shop. My previous boss always looked out for me, and a few years later he lost the lease hold of his new place. He didn't want to start another business, so he came to work part time in my shop. It was quite funny and we shared many jokes because he was now working for me, things like "now it's your turn to get the brushes!" I think that's real barbering – people working together and having fun, no matter what.

After I had my shop I did many courses and learnt a lot, we were always improving which made me study more. I've always had a love of education, and I think I am probably the female barber who has travelled round the world teaching the most. I don't know anyone else like this; you don't see many on social media. However I don't have the City & Guilds certificate – because of the language barrier it is very hard for me to answer any written questions. I would say it is a weak part of my career, but I do believe that education is the key to success. This is why I started the Barbersclan project, which many other barbers help and support with.

Barbering in Brazil still suffers from too little education. This is why I turned a property I own into the Barbersclan Academy, where people can stay for 2 days studying courses with barbers from all over. We have education, BBQs, guitar playing... it's a lot of fun. I think barbering isn't only about techniques but also how to be a strong part of your community. The barbershop is a very powerful place, so communication is as important as skill in cutting hair. This is the reason for Barbersclan Academy. I got the name from a teacher in Scotland who told me that a clan is a strong chain of people who have similarities and a family bond. It was the perfect name as we are a clan of barbers!

I created the *Revista QG* magazine because I was aware of the lack of education in Brazil and felt that barbers here could benefit from seeing work from abroad, as well as from their own country. I was lucky to have Willian who is great with design. The idea started as a book, but we felt we would be limited and not everyone would read it, so making a magazine was suggested. There were no magazines in Portuguese, even though there are a lot of industry publications in UK and USA. We wanted to show the Brazil's style. We've been lucky to have a lot of barbers really happy to help, especially since the first issue went out.

Before we knew it, the magazine was going out in Brazil, Portugal and Italy. If it was in English it would've been too difficult as it's not my or Willian's first language. We hope with the help of barbers from all over the world we can continue to make it bigger. There are other magazines but I don't see this as a competition. It's always good to share the knowledge we have as barbers. The goal was to help explore the business, let people know what is going on, and provide a little bit of education with each issue.

Where do I see myself in the industry? I am no more than a barber who loves to be on the shop floor, no more than that. My experience and love for the trade define me as a shop floor barber, but my country is so poor when it comes to technique and education that it has made me try to educate a bit more. That's why we're doing classes and connecting with the right people, to make the base a bit stronger in Brazil. I love being a regular barber on the shop floor and I don't need more than that"

The 'Barber Boom'

"As I mentioned before I worked with the best barbers in the centre of Coventry, and we were always looking for new stuff. About 13 or so years ago there was nothing around – even when we went to Salon International there were maybe one or 2 stands for barbering. If there were barber-related stands we would jump at the chance to see what they were doing, but we also used to check out all the hairdressing ones too. Eventually we would get bored of it however, as it's another world.

Year after year, things started to change – like when Chris Foster began showing off haircuts. He's great every time I see him, even now. Nowadays barbering is everywhere! It's the same with shops – when I opened mine it was the only one in the area. Now they're all over in Coventry, we even have them in the supermarket! The problem is the barbers are often not trained or qualified. The demand is so high that they will employ anyone. In a way I guess it's good as it creates job opportunities, and there's more than enough business to go round (especially as our customers are very loyal). I've had clients stray in the past, and they soon return to our shop as they like the experience and technique of our barbers.

To ensure we stay above the rest there needs to be constant learning. Men's hair is huge and it is causing a big change in the industry, for example the Toni&Guy Academy in Coventry has closed down as they lost a lot of the market. This is because more men are going to barbershops. Men are making this change because a lot more barbers are fully trained. They can do the disconnections and the classics, they give a great finish, and they're cheaper than someone like Toni&Guy. The big academies now have the men's courses and they're in demand.

I would say it has been improving and expanding for the last 15 years, but it has been in the last 2 years that there has been a huge boom in the UK. In Brazil it's the same. The last 2 years have shown a massive increase, and the big companies and the rich are taking advantage of it. For example, in Brazil it's often the people who have chains of bars or restaurants that are now opening chains of barbershops! There have been plenty of big entrepreneurs investing a lot. They have decided it's a great way to make money, so they're opening big barbershops with pubs and restaurants inside them as well. They are beautiful, but they are just places to cut hair. They don't have any atmosphere. I feel it's my job to bring a bit of the real barber shop culture to Brazil. As I said before, I feel blessed by my past in barbering – to have an English boss with 35 years of experience to teach me to become a proper barber. Not an arrogant person, but someone who respects their customers and shares their lives with their clients, making their shops a welcoming community. There isn't the same culture of barbering here, but I feel with Barbersclan we can move towards it. Barbering was a dying trade a few years ago, and now it's growing so much it is crazy. I think with the right education we can go even further.

In the next 5 years I think we will see a lot of standardisation. There will be more shops but the ones that are under qualified will close their doors. There are also a lot of brands on the market right now, I think some will become stable and others will fade. More education will be needed. As the market grows so will the competition.

I think the hairdressing world has changed their opinion about us, before we were seen as butchers. I visited the Sassoon Academy for classes, and they kept saying that barbers do things the wrong way. It felt a bit mean. Now I think people's views of barbering is changing. We're improving slowly, but we're definitely doing a better job now!"

Healthy Competition

"When it comes to competitions and titles I'm not particularly keen on them, but I do have some. When I worked in Paris I won an award and in 2016 and 2017 I was named Master Barber of the Year for Brazil. I also won an award for the Foreign Trade Barber of the Year. Competitions are great when they provide opportunities to become platform artists or educators, helping people to find different directions in the industry. It's good for the general public because the images created give clients ideas and move trends forward. It makes our industry feel more alive.

On the other hand, sometimes competitions can create big egos for barbers who don't necessarily have much experience. They may have done this one haircut in one style, spent a lot of time on it, mastered it, and then won a title. They have this title forever, and feel this is all they need. Overall there are good and bad things about competitions. Barbering is about techniques and education, but also about behaviour. Maybe there should be a book about how to behave – especially after winning –some could benefit from it."

The Power of Social Media

"I don't have a good knowledge of social media. Sometimes I post, sometimes I don't. I know what I like, but I think at some point I will need help with my accounts. Some things I post are for certain types of barbers and don't match what I'm doing in the shop. My social media at the moment is not only for work, it is personal too. I have followers from shanty towns in Brazil because I teach and work with them, but the style from the shop is not the sort of thing they would use. That makes it all a bit messy for me, you know?

I still think it is great, for some people. It has made them massive names, the biggest names in barbering. Not only because of their work, but also because of their knowledge of social media. If you want to sell yourself online, you need to use your social media to get to your customers not the competition, so remember that when you look at people to add. To get more business we need to look at local businesses and people to get them in our shops. Personally I really need to study it more to use it better."

Any Advice?

"Never ever give up learning. We have a date to start, but we don't have a date to finish. Sometimes we need courses, sometimes we need demonstrations, and sometimes we need to work on new skills. If my plan was to be in the UK barbering, I'd look at more English classes.

We also have to sometimes go outside of barbering to learn. We need to remember that we're no better than anyone else. We all have different knowledge and different experience. I just try to give what I know. I would say to young barbers: be yourself, find your own path, be different, and make the barbering trade part of the community again. Learn to respect and honour your clients too, it's so important. The younger generation is so important to the future of the industry, and having the ability to look after your clientele is integral.

Projects like The Lions Barber Collective are great for everyone; it'll have a positive effect on the world. The next generation of barbers have the potential to make a huge difference, having things like the internet and all the barber shows, it will make things progress much faster than previous generations. I hope that everyone takes advantage of what is now available, and as I said, never stop learning."

@sindidevitte

I hope Sindi's final piece of advice resonates with both the young and experienced barbers of the world. Learning is fundamental to success, no matter what your age or experience. The barbers I visited in Sao Paulo were incredible, unlike any I've seen in the UK. Their hunger to learn was unreal. On the final day of the

159

course we finished cutting at 4pm and made our way outside for a real Brazilian BBQ (which was the best steak I have ever eaten) and when I went back inside the academy to visit the bathroom some of the guys were still cutting each others hair. I couldn't resist and got stuck in myself. We grew in numbers and we were cutting each others hair until gone midnight. Their thirst for knowledge and experience was brilliant. It's interesting to hear of the crossover Sindi mentions, with unrelated businesses starting their own high-end chains. It's a trend that hasn't happened in the UK as yet – but who knows what the future holds.

Pretty much everyone I've spoken to loves being behind that chair – it's our base and helps us to grow. I always feel like when I'm cutting hair, it's almost like time off. Sindi seems to feel the same. After spending 16 years on the shop floor she's a veteran who's been around long before the current 'barber boom', however she's only been fully recognised in the last few years. This is a great example for anyone who aspires to do all the other great things Sindi has achieved; things take time so be patient. It takes a long time to master anything worth mastering.

Sindi's interview made me think back to the beginnings of my career. Perhaps there was more barbering than I originally thought. I guess I was too distracted by hairdressing at the time. I'm also very much in agreement with her prediction that the over saturation of the market will cause only the skilled barbers to survive. Not only that, shops will need to create an environment people will enjoy and a culture of retention, as well as employing sound business management to keep their heads above the water. That doesn't just go for new shops, complacency kills, and even established locations will have to ensure they keep up.

Knowing your target audience is so important. We spend a lot of time looking at our competition and building global status, when we should spend more time drumming up local business. Our customers pay for the food on our tables, so unless you're in the world of education it's wise to start looking closer to home for followers. Sindi's issue when it comes to having 2 different markets to cater for may be solved by multiple accounts, but that's hard to keep up with. A lot of salon owners have chosen to hire someone to run their accounts, which can help to ensure your presence grows in the correct way.

One thing that Sindi said when I was in Brazil that really resonated with me was "Your client is King, look after their crown". She said it when discussing leaving the hair on a clients crown longer to help with control and ease of styling for your client. However she said it with passion and this statement shows she's all about helping people, whether they be her clients in the chair or the barbers of Brazil. She is one of the most committed and dedicated people I've met in the industry, and was the perfect end to this journey.

TC

New Beginnings
&
Final Thoughts

New Beginnings

As my journey to Brazil comes to an end, so does this book. Beginning in an airport and ending in one seemed fitting, and this past year and the people I've met have taught me a great deal about this profession, and about myself.

Finishing such an incredible trip has further instilled in me how lucky I am to be part of one of the oldest trades in the world. I've travelled countless miles and visited several countries, each with its own unique approach to barbering and their own views on the industry. These experiences and the people I've met have shaped me, and I think it's important to accept that your beliefs and attitudes are going to evolve the more you learn. My last trip to Brazil was no different; the barbers here were welcoming, friendly, and had a keen desire to learn – something we can take for granted in the UK where have many facilities to help us improve. On that occasion when the course finished at 4pm we were up till midnight cutting hair, and the students were happy to commit this time, no problem. There are a huge amount of barbers in South America, and from the 150 or so that I was lucky enough to meet, their willingness to learn leads me to believe that the barber boom is growing in Brazil too.

Now that I'm making my way back to the UK, it really resonates with me that I've come to the end of the journey I've taken with this book. I'm incredibly fortunate to have been met with co-operation, patience, and time from all the individuals I've met along the way. Time is a precious commodity, and I thank them for allowing me to use theirs. My hope is that with the combined years of experience and knowledge, you the reader can hopefully learn as much as I have. There were times I thought I may not be able to finish, that this book and all these stories would be forgotten about. First and foremost I am a barber, and with running my business, teaching, founding a charity, and having a young family to take care of, I was worried the book would fall by the wayside. I guess it being here is proof that if you put your mind to something, nothing can stop you. I try to make the most of every opportunity (such as writing thousands of words in an airport lounge) and I hope I can continue to do this throughout my career and life. We spend a lot of time talking about what we want to do, but consistency, dedication, and commitment are the only way to make your dream a reality.

Coming to the end of this book has led me not only to reflect on the answers my interviewees have given me, but also on my opinion. I chose to ask each person the same, formulaic questions, and I guess it's only fair I do the same.

Backstory

I've been in the industry since I was 18, so 15 years this year. I'm lucky to have found something I love and stumbled on it by chance with a helpful nudge from my family, for which I am ever grateful. There's over a 100 years of experience in this book and I've learnt more throughout this process than ever before. It's also indicated to me there's still so much to know, and I'm coming to terms with the facts I'll never learn it all.

Throughout my career I've been lucky enough to be associated with some huge brands, and because of this I've had wonderful experiences all over the world. I am an ambassador for Fit For Vikings Beard Care, Hunt & Hustle Scissors, Exeter College Hair Department, The Bluebeards Revenge, and most recently I've been given the opportunity to become a Global Ambassador and launch the brand new 1922 by JM Keune across the globe from Russia to The States and everywhere in between. I'm proud to have the opportunity to represent each and every one of these companies.

Since the beginning of this book, my career has continued to grow to heights I never believed possible. Last month I was onstage at the top floor of the Amsterdam Tower, unveiling the new men's range from Keune in front of all their global distributors from 70 countries. It was slightly surreal and such an honour to be a part of. I'm now looking forward to the next adventure with Keune and hope this is the start of special.

I also sit on the Industry board for the City&Guilds Barbering NVQ , something which I still pinch myself over. Sitting in a room with all those great minds is always an incredible experience and I've learnt a lot from them.

I'm extremely lucky to hold such prestigious roles – especially when it comes to education. I see education as the future of this industry. It can help to revitalise, standardise, and develop barbering to help it reach new heights. Nearly every person I've spoken to in this book realises that if you want to progress, be part of the 'barber boom', or even just stay relative, you need to be constantly learning, evolving and appreciate that you'll never know it all.

The 'Barber Boom

The rise in barbering has been coming for a long time now, long before I started my hair journey. As Carl Blake pointed out he was aware of this beginnings of the 'barber boom' before I'd even picked up my first ever Wahl Super Tapers! The likes of David Beckham and the metrosexual movement is when things really started to get moving. At this time a lot of men went to hairdressers not barbers for their cuts, as hairdressers popularised the use of straighteners and colour for men's hair. This was groundbreaking at the time, and really pushed men into the habit of self-grooming. This was the first step which created a culture and formed a habit of personal grooming that eventually evolved into what we see today.

Another thing that has really effected barbering in recent years is the popularity of fades. This trend came to us from the USA, thanks to Afro barbershops. The UK barbers took to this very quickly thanks to the confidence they have in their clippers. Fading is traditionally a skill barbers not hairdressers had, and as such it resulted in a demand for skilled barbers who knew the style. Men that had developed the habit of grooming at salons wanted the faded cuts and it wouldn't have taken many visits to their hairdresser to realise they weren't practiced in this skill. The only place to get this done was at the barbershop. This created a much bigger market for barbers than in the past. Alan Beak realised what was happening and combined the fade with European styles and cuts, drawing inspiration from the past.

This new trend led to more attention, press, and money being introduced into the profession. Publications were started, products were created, and there were events and trade shows – all of which began to be popularised on social media. We are now in a world where we have better clippers, scissors, magazines, education, and events than ever before, and are incredibly lucky to be a part of such a phenomenon. A subculture began to develop in these beginning years of the boom which has grown immeasurably – there's even a barber look and style. Barbering was beginning to be seen as cool, and there was more and more attention being given to the art of cutting and styling men's hair. We as barbers have created a new sub culture, all of our own. With this rise the industry has managed to evolve, with courses being offered to teach techniques that meet the demand of the modern man.

The industry will continue to improve as long as there is a need for it. I know for a fact that the 2 biggest clipper brands out there are always evolving and refining their tools, partly to outdo each other. With newcomers like JRL USA coming to the market place things are starting to get even more interesting. This is great for us as barbers, but our clients are the biggest winners of all. Lines are becoming blurred between what a barber and a hairstylist is, and the field as a whole is giving more respect to the skill it takes to specialise in men's hair.

In 5 years' time barbering will still be relevant, however it will have changed and developed into something different. There will still be classic, old school barbers (there's always a market for them), as well as more 'modern' shops which will offer a variety of men's grooming services. I recently saw a shop advertising a colour specialist which only further proves my theory that the industry is changing, providing more services than in the past. This will help to drive barbering forward, eventually being on equal footing with hair salons.

Then comes the question of over saturation. Like Mark Peyton said, the work ethic will separate those who have the passion and those who don't, leaving the best to rise to the top.

The weak skilled and less committed will fall away leaving the more advanced, prepared barbers to continue.

In the past year I've spoken with salons all over the world who want to integrate barbering into their locations, so perhaps that might be where a part of the future lies. Far from being a small skill set, barbering will be pushed to involve more techniques with regards to colour, products and styling. This could be in their own shops or in merged salons. Whatever the future holds, it's great that we're pushing boundaries and finally gaining the respect barbering deserves.

Products, Tools, Publications, & Events

Throughout my career things have changed a lot when it comes to products and tools. When I began clippers were seen as cheating, whereas now every class I teach is full of hairdressers wanting to know how to use them. Combine that with the rise in barbershops, and the amount of professionals demanding clippers has gone through the roof! More customers mean more and better products. It has also created competition between brands, with each one constantly developing and driving forward to produce better, more efficient tools. We now have a choice of high quality tools that are always improving, which make our jobs easier.

Andis and Wahl have been battling it out at the top for the last few years always looking for something new and exciting for us barbers. This competition can only be a good thing. Every year there are multiple new clipper and trimmer models on the market and I've been lucky enough to even help with trials and development of some models. It's very exciting; who doesn't like trying out a new set of clippers?

Then there are scissors. Recent years suggest barbers don't know how to use them with the same skill as clippers, so courses are becoming more popular, creating a demand for tools in this field specifically for barbering. I've worked with the leaders in this department, Hunt & Hustle. They've created one of the best pairs of scissors I've ever used in my career, their Ace of Spades.

Finally, products. Never have there been so many male-only brands on the market. You even have a lot of barbershops selling their own ranges, helping to design, create, and brand it – like Reuzel for example. There are also long-standing brands (such as American Crew) which are still thriving. It's great for the industry because there's a huge variety, which helps to create countless styles for different hair types and preferences. Long gone are the days of barbershops using Dax Wax and pharmacy-bought, cheap gels. The big guys are getting on board with the 'barber boom' too. As I mentioned I've been working with Keune for the global launch of their 1922 men's range. They are globally established in over 70 countries, having been around for 95 years, yet it is only now they are launching a true men's range. This is a sign the hair world has taken notice. The fact that the men's grooming industry was worth over $81 billion in 2016 and has yet another growth of 3% in 2017 speak volumes."

Healthy Competition

I believe in using competitions as a platform to project people into the limelight and give people experience – especially with live barber battle finals. I've been a part of a few and they've definitely helped me overcome my anxiety, as well as helping me to grow as a presenter and educator. I love the way Jonathan from El Patron likened them to our version of sports, I suppose like he said it's the nearest thing we as a sub culture have.

Whether the barber wins or not is unimportant. Sam Wall put it best when he said it's not about winning or losing, just learning – and that comes from a guy who has a fair few titles! His wins are not why he has succeeded. Sure, they're a part of his journey but I've known barbers to win multiple awards and go on to do not much else. I've also know barbers to lose and then become brand ambassadors or global educators. There are barbers who've never entered a competition, but travel the world earning a great living. So the long and short of it is that competitions are good for the industry and encourage growth and diversity, but they're not the be all and end all of someone's career.

The title of best barber can't really be judged by a photo or one-off, live final. It should take into account their customer service, quality of work over a longer period of time, and what they've given back to the industry. Competition winning can be a part of your success, but the individual determines the direction. Once again drawing from Mark Peyton, perhaps we should look for 'inspirational barbers' instead.

The Power of Social Media

Social media has aided me a great deal in terms of both my professional and social life. Being outside of London or another big city is no longer the disadvantage it once was. Clients often ask me if I'm interested in moving to London but I don't believe it's necessary. With the globalisation that using social media correctly provides, you can network and make contacts whether your barbershop is in London, New York or Torquay.

Social Media is an incredibly important tool for any type of business, but it needs to be used correctly – this is relevant to life as a whole, not just barbering. It can be a huge distraction and a way of procrastinating and time-wasting. Mindlessly scrolling for hours through your feed is not an effective use of your time, but promoting your business or using it for inspiration and research is. There's so much knowledge right at your fingertips but you have to stay focused. It's also extremely important to ensure any online content about you or your business is something positive and that you're proud of, as its accessible forever.

Any Advice?

It's been a goal of mine throughout these interviews to draw out wisdom, opinions and ideas from barbers all around the world. I wanted to have a variety of different types of people in the industry, from educators to business owners and award-winners. My hope being that even if just a few people read their advice and take it on board, I'd have done my job. I always tell my students that if they can take even just one thing from a workshop, it's a success. These experiences help shape us into the people we're going to be, both professionally and in our personal lives. Learn from experiences, from mistakes; use them to push yourself and you'll be surprised what you can achieve

Never stop learning. I'm a huge believer in the marginal gains theory, it's all about improving on smaller skills over time, which combine to result in advances overall. To paraphrase Walt Disney, everything matters – even the finest details. Use your mistakes as a way to move forward, don't ignore them. Growth comes from failure and it's ok to feel lost at first but it's vital to address it and move on. Surround yourself with those you admire because you're a product of your environment. Spend your time with successful people in all aspects of your life and be around individuals who challenge you. I've learnt so much since working alongside the guys I've interviewed in this book, and I still have so much to know.

Being true to yourself and having some integrity will go a long way. If you want to work with people then be nice, hardworking, and easy to get along with. If you get the opportunity to work with someone in platform work or editorial, if you prove to be difficult, then it's highly unlikely you'll be rehired. This hinders your reputation and prevents you from progressing. With the internet the world has become a small place and everyone is in touch with one another, so always be kind and of course, work to the best of your ability – you never know who might be watching. The reason I'm working with Keune now is thanks to an event at their headquarters in Amsterdam. When the show had finished there was an after party and while everyone else partied, I spent my time with the Keune team members discussing hair, showing them my #th13teen collection and talking about my love of barbering. Since that day I've been in constant contact with company. Never underestimate your actions now when it comes to opportunities in the future, after all it's not who you know, it's who knows you!

Always try to exceed expectations rather than simply satisfy them, and finally nice guys don't finish last, they finish first.

Final Thoughts

It's amazing really but with no intention the journey of this book has come full circle as I start my journey, once again to the States for another barber led trip. This time with clipper company JRL USA and to sunny Florida a little over a year since I started this book. I have had a lot of experiences and learnt a lot from them and all these amazing interviews, coming to some kind of conclusions. No surprise here but I bet the 'barber boom' is here to stay – for a while at least. Fashions always dictate the market and we're beginning to see a trend towards longer hair and away from the fades that have dominated the industry of late, suggesting a change in the service clients will want. The demand will be there all the same and luckily now barbers have the network and education to evolve with the changing styles.

The continuing rise in men's grooming can only be a good thing for our industry, and so far it has led to amazing development of new products, tools, and skills, creating competition and innovation which stands to only advance barbering as a trade and a business. This interest and heightened awareness of the profession has already lent itself to encouraging standardisation and requiring higher skill levels than before. The hair industry has dramatically changed it's attitude towards barbering, recognising the skill and precision it requires.

There is one thing that is apparent from all these interviews with barbers from all over the globe…we're all different. We all have different drives, opinions, skills, and priorities. It takes all types of barber to create the culture we know and love. My thoughts are once you find your call in barbering, look a little deeper and find your niche within it. This allows you to stand out in the ever-growing crowd. Once you have found your forte (make sure it is something you enjoy, otherwise it'll be hard to maintain.) work at it. Spend your free time between clients doing it, on your commute, or after hours study it. If you're consistent you'll carve yourself out a place, just as the people in this book have. This could be anything from your own podcast to a YouTube channel, blog, or photography. Find what you love in our fantastic industry and become a vital part of the 'barber boom'. Help us to keep pushing it forward.

It's a very exciting time to be part of the barbering world, and I can't wait to see where the future takes us, no matter where it may be. As the internet has facilitated more communication, the opportunities are endless. The next generation of barbers are in good stead to take the industry to the next level, and I'm thrilled to see where their creativity will take them.

The last 6 years since I opened my own salon have been a massive learning curve, and I've been fortunate enough to be a part of this huge growth. The 'barber boom' is most definitely alive and well, and will continue for the foreseeable future if the barbers continue to educate themselves and evolve – especially as huge international hairdressing brands take notice. I consider myself very lucky to be part of the hair industry, always have, but to be part of it right now is incredible. Being accepted into the profession was a wonderful experience for me – especially as I came from a hairdressing background. In the 1920's, the barbershop was an institution and I hope the 2020's will continue to revive that community ethos and see barbers go from strength to strength. We have to look ourselves and and each other to ensure we step into the next decade leading the way in the hair industry.

I cannot thank everyone who has been a part of this book enough, and it has shown me that 'barber love' is much more than just a hash tag, it's something we can live by. Here's to an incredible profession, the 'barber boom', and an exciting future.